Write it in
FRENCH

By

CHRISTOPHER KENDRIS

B.S., M.S., Columbia University
in the City of New York
M.A., Ph.D., Northwestern University
in Evanston, Illinois
Diplômé, Faculté des Lettres, Université de Paris
(en Sorbonne)
et Institut de Phonétique, Paris

Formerly Assistant Professor
Department of French and Spanish
State University of New York
Albany, New York

BARRON'S EDUCATIONAL SERIES, INC.

For my family with love

All inquiries should be addressed to:
Barron's Educational Series, Inc.
250 Wireless Boulevard
Hauppauge, New York 11788

Library of Congress Catalog Card No. 90-670
International Standard Book No. 4361-8

Library of Congress Cataloging in Publication Data
Kendris, Christopher.
    Write it in French / by Christopher Kendris.
        p.   cm.—(Barron's teach-yourself books)
    "Adapted from Beginning to Write in French"—
T.p. verso.
    ISBN 0-8120-4361-8
    1. French language—Textbooks for foreign speakers—
English. 2. French language—Self-instruction. I. Kendris,
Christopher. Beginning to Write in French. II. Title. III. Series.
PC2129.E5K45 1990
448.2'421—dc20   90-670
                                                    CIP

PRINTED IN THE UNITED STATES OF AMERICA

90 510 9

Contents

Appendix

About the author

◆

Christopher Kendris has worked as interpreter and translator for the U.S. State Department at the American Embassy in Paris.

Dr. Kendris earned his B.S. and M.S. degrees at Columbia University in the City of New York, where he held a New York State scholarship, and his M.A. and Ph.D. degrees at Northwestern University in Evanston, Illinois. He also earned two diplomas with *Mention très Honorable* at the Université de Paris (en Sorbonne), Faculté des Lettres, Ecole Supérieure de Préparation et de Perfectionnement des Professeurs de Français à l'Etranger, and at the Institut de Phonétique, Paris.

He has taught French at the College of The University of Chicago as visiting summer lecturer and at Northwestern University, where he held a Teaching Assistantship and Tutorial Fellowship for four years. He has also taught at Colby College, Duke University, Rutgers—The State University of New Jersey, and the State University of New York at Albany. He was Chairman of the Foreign Languages Department at Farmingdale High School, Farmingdale, New York, where he was also a teacher of French and Spanish.

He is the author of numerous modern language books and workbooks published by Barron's Educational Series, Inc., including *301* and *501 French Verbs, 301* and *501 Spanish Verbs, French Now* (a Level One worktext), *Spanish Now, Book II,* and *How to Prepare for the College Board Achievement Test in French* and *Spanish, French the Easy Way,* and *Spanish the Easy Way.*

In 1986 he was one of ninety-five American high school teachers of foreign languages across the United States who was honored with a Rockefeller Foundation Fellowship in a competition that included about 1,000 candidates. The Fellowship gave him the opportunity to study new teaching methods and techniques at the Pedagogical Institute at the International School of French Language and Civilization at the Alliance Française in Paris. He was one of only four winners in New York State.

Dr. Christopher Kendris is listed in *Contemporary Authors.*

Introduction

This book contains new techniques and exercises to help you improve your skill in writing French simply. If you use this book with a desire to practice, from the first page to the last, you will be able to raise your level of competence from basic to superior provided, of course, that you have some elementary knowledge of the French language.

What I kept in mind constantly while writing this book is your need to get a higher score on the writing sections of the New York State Regents examinations, the Second Language Proficiency examinations, and all other standardized examinations that test your skill in writing simple French.

There are forty assignments in this book. Each one consists of five idioms, expressions, or words that are among those on the level of competence tested on the New York State Regents examination. Each assignment is related in thought so that a situation or image is created. This arrangement makes it interesting for you and makes it easier to retain the vocabulary in each topic. After every three assignments there is a review test, except for the last test, which covers the last four units. The idioms, expressions, and words have been numbered consecutively for convenience in referring to them.

At the end of this book there are several sections that contain basic review material. Take a few minutes right now to browse through the Table of Contents and the Appendix. You will find useful material to review or to learn for the first time.

Here are some highlights in this new book.

1. Each *devoir* is on a topic people enjoy talking or writing about.

2. Practical situations are put into action so they become meaningful.

3. You will have a chance to write lists of words or expressions in French for such things as grocery and shopping lists, telephone messages, items you would take with you on vacation, and many others. You need this kind of practice because the new Second Language Proficiency exams require you to write such lists.

4. The personal topics will motivate you to write about yourself or someone else and to list words to describe yourself or other persons.

5. There are situations where you will have to write a few words in French to persuade someone, to get and give information, to socialize, or to write simple notes or post cards to friends.

6. The French idiomatic expressions, verbs, and words in this book are used all the time in daily life. Whatever you want to say, here is your chance to write it in French! There are also drawings that give you an opportunity to write a few words about them in French.

7. The writing exercises are designed in such a way as to get you to express your feelings with confidence and power in every written word. They will motivate you to open up your thoughts and write them in simple French. As long as you make yourself understood, that is what is important. After all, language is communication when you hear it, speak it, or write it.

8. The Appendix in the back pages of the book contains sections on antonyms and synonyms, a review of basic vocabulary by topics, a review of basic French idioms, and other features that will help you to do your best when you want to write something simple in French.

9. Finally, I have included twenty-three basic French verbs fully conjugated in all the tenses so you can refer to that section from time to time when you are writing in French.

I sincerely hope that you get a lot out of this book and that you enjoy using it as much as I enjoyed writing it for you. But, remember, you will get out of this book whatever you put into it. Now, let's begin! Write it in French!

Christopher Kendris
B.S., M.S., M.A., Ph.D.

Je m'appelle _____
(My name is)

C'est aujourd'hui _____
(Today is)

(lundi, mardi, mercredi, jeudi, vendredi, samedi, dimanche)
(Monday, Tuesday, Wednesday, Thursday, Friday, Saturday, Sunday)

le _____
(premier, deux, etc.)   **(septembre, octobre, etc.)**
(first, second, etc.)   (September, October, etc.)

Qui est-ce?—C'est moi.

(Who is it?)—(It's me.)

I.   Write a brief sentence of your own in French using the expression given. If you are not ready to do that, just copy the model sentence for practice.

1. **s'appeler**   to be named, called   **Je m'appelle . . .**
My name is . . .

_____

2. **avoir . . . ans**   to be . . . years old   **J'ai dix-sept ans.**
I am seventeen years old.

_____

3. **se lever**   to get up   **Je me lève à six heures et demie.**
I get up at six thirty.

_____

4. **tous les matins**   every morning   **Tous les matins je prends un bon petit déjeuner.**
Every morning I have a good breakfast.

_____

5. **donner sur**   to look out on,   **La salle à manger donne sur le jardin.**
to face   The dining room faces the garden.

_____

II.   On the line write in French one word that will make the sentence meaningful and grammatically correct. Refer to the model sentences in Exercise **I** above if you need to.

1. **Je m'** _____ **Robert.**

2. **J'** _____ **dix-sept ans.**

3. **Je me** _____ **à six heures et demie.**

4. **Tous les** _____ **je prends un bon petit déjeuner.**

5. **La salle à manger** _____ **sur le jardin.**

III. Answer the following questions in French in complete sentences.

1. **Comment vous appelez-vous?** _____

_____

2. **Quel âge avez-vous?** _____

_____

3. **A quelle heure est-ce que vous vous levez tous les matins?** _____

_____

IV. Write at least three sentences in French about yourself. Refer to Exercises **I, II, III** above.

_____

_____

_____

V. On the line write in French what the person is doing.

Le garçon boit du lait.   **Que fait-il?**
(What is he doing?)

Il _____

VI. Change one letter in any part of the word and get another French word.
Example: **chevaux** (horses) Change **a** to **e** and you get: **cheveux** (hair)

se laver (to wash oneself) _____ (to get up)

VII. Add one letter in any part of the word and get another French word.
Example: **avoir** (to have) Add **s** and you get: **savoir** (to know)

frais (fresh, cool) _____ (strawberry)

VIII. Write three words in French that are things you eat or drink for breakfast.

1. _____ 2. _____ 3. _____

IX. How many French words can you find in the word **MAISON?** Write at least six.

┌─────────────────────┐
│ **M A I S O N** │
└─────────────────────┘

1. _____ 3. _____ 5. _____

2. _____ 4. _____ 6. _____

X. Write two verbs in French stating what you do. They are in this lesson.

1. *Je* _____ 2. *Je* _____

Je m'appelle _____

C'est aujourd'hui _____

le _____

Les quatre saisons de l'année

(The four seasons of the year)

I. Write a brief sentence of your own in French using the expression given. If you are not ready to do that, just copy the model sentence for practice.

6. **faire chaud**   to be warm (weather)   **Il fait chaud en été.**
It is warm in summer.

_____

7. **faire froid**   to be cold (weather)   **Il fait froid en hiver.**
It is cold in winter.

_____

8. **faire beau**   to be beautiful (weather)   **Il fait beau au printemps.**
It is beautiful in the spring.

_____

9. **faire frais**   to be cool (weather)   **Il fait frais en automne.**
It is cool in autumn.

_____

10. **faire doux**   to be nice (weather)   **Il fait doux aujourd'hui. Je vais au parc.**
It's nice today. I'm going to the park.

_____

II. On the line write in French one word that will make the sentence meaningful and grammatically correct. Refer to the model sentences in Exercise **I** above if you need to.

1. **Il _____ chaud en été.**

2. **Il fait _____ en hiver.**

3. **Il fait beau au _____ .**

4. **Il fait frais _____ automne.**

5. **Il fait doux _____ .**

III. Answer the following questions in French in complete sentences. [Quel temps fait-il? *What's the weather like?*]

    1. **Quel temps fait-il en été?** _____

    2. **Quel temps fait-il en hiver?** _____

    3. **Quel temps fait-il au printemps?** _____

    4. **Quel temps fait-il en automne?** _____

    5. **Quel temps fait-il aujourd'hui? Où allez-vous?** _____

_____

IV. Write six sentences in French. Tell what the weather is like in autumn, in winter, in the spring and in summer. Also tell what the weather is like today and where you are going. Refer to Exercises **I**, **II** and **III** above.

_____

_____

_____

_____

_____

_____

V. On the line write in French what the person is doing.

Le garçon lit un livre.

Que fait-il?
(What is he doing?)

Il _____

VI. Change one letter in any part of the word and get another French word.
Example: **Que** (what) Change **e** to **i** and you get: **Qui** (who, whom)

fait Change this word to: _____ (milk)

VII. Take out one letter in any part of the word and get another French word.
Example: **dans** (in) Take out **d** and you get: **ans** (years)

lait (milk) _____ (is reading)

VIII. Write three words in French pertaining to the weather.

    1. _____ 2. _____ 3. _____

IX. How many French words can you find in the word **LAIT**? Write at least three.

$$\boxed{\text{L A I T}}$$

    1. _____ 2. _____ 3. _____

X. Write one French word to complete the thought in the following sentence.

Je vais au parc parce qu'il fait _____ **aujourd'hui.**

4 Les quatre saisons de l'année

Qu'est-ce que j'aime faire?

(What do I like to do?)

I. Write a brief sentence of your own in French using the expression given. If you are not ready to do that, just copy the model sentence for practice.

11. **pleuvoir**   to rain   **Quand il pleut, je reste à la maison.**
When it rains I stay at home.

_____

12. **neiger**   to snow   **Quand il neige je vais au parc.**
When it snows I go to the park.

_____

13. **se promener**   to take a walk   **J'aime me promener dans le parc quand il neige.**
I like to take a walk in the park when it snows.

_____

14. **chez moi**   to (at) my house, home   **J'aime lire chez moi quand il pleut.**
I like to read at home when it rains.

_____

15. **en plein air**   outdoors, in the open   **J'aime être en plein air quand il fait beau.**
I like to be outdoors when the weather is pleasant.

_____

II. On the line write in French one word that will make the sentence meaningful and grammatically correct. Refer to the model sentences in Exercise **I** above if you need to.

1. **Quand** _____ **pleut, je reste à la maison.**

2. **Quand il** _____ **, je vais au parc.**

3. **J'aime** _____ **promener dans le parc quand il neige.**

4. **J'aime lire chez** _____ **quand il pleut.**

5. **J'aime être en plein** _____ **quand il fait beau.**

III. Answer the following questions in French in complete sentences.

1. **Que faites-vous quand il pleut?** _____

_____

2. **Que faites-vous quand il neige?** _____

_____

3. **Qu'est-ce que vous aimez faire dans un parc?** _____

_____

4. **Nommez les quatre saisons de l'année.** _____

_____

5. **En quelle saison est-ce qu'il neige?** _____

_____

IV. Write five sentences in French telling what you do when it rains, what you do when it snows, what you like to do in a park when it snows, what you like to do at home when it rains, and where you like to be when the weather is pleasant. Refer to Exercises **I, II** and **III** above.

_____

_____

_____

_____

_____

V. On the line write in French what the person is doing.

La jeune fille danse.

Que fait-elle?
(What is she doing?)

Elle _____

VI. Add two letters in any part of the word and get another French word.

air (air) _____ (to do, to make)

VII. Add one letter in any part of the word and get another French word.

moi (me) _____ (month)

VIII. Write two verbs in the present indicative tense using **je** as the subject. They must pertain to two things that you do.

1. _____ 2. _____

IX. The words in the following sentence are scrambled. Write them in the correct word order.

Le / lait / du / garçon / boit. _____

X. Write two French words to complete the thought in the following sentence.

J'aime _____ **promener dans le parc quand il** _____.

Je m'appelle _____

C'est aujourd'hui _____

le _____

I. Write at least four sentences in French about yourself.

_____

_____

_____

_____

II. Write at least four sentences in French about the seasons of the year.

_____

_____

_____

_____

III. Write four sentences in French telling what you do when it rains, what you do when it snows, where you go when the weather is nice and what you do in a park.

_____

_____

_____

_____

IV. Complete the following sentences by writing in French words that will make the statements meaningful.

1. **Je me** _____ **à six heures et demie.**

2. **Tous les** _____ **je prends un** _____ **petit déjeuner.**

3. **Il fait** _____ **en hiver et il fait** _____ **en été.**

4. **Au printemps il** _____ **beau.**

V. You are going shopping. In French, write a list of things you plan to buy.

1. _____ 2. _____ 3. _____

VI. On the line write in French what the person is doing.

1.

Que fait-il?

_____

2.

Que fait-elle?

_____

3.

Que fait-il?

_____

VII. Change one letter in any part of the word and get another French word.

se laver (to wash oneself) _____ (to get up)

VIII. Add one letter in any part of the word and get another French word.

frais (fresh, cool) _____ (strawberry)

IX. Take out one letter in any part of the word and get another French word.

danse _____ (in)

X. How many French words can you find in the word **DANSE?** Write at least three.

$$\boxed{\text{D A N S E}}$$

1. _____ 2. _____ 3. _____

proverbe **Qui se ressemble s'assemble.** Birds of a feather flock together.

Je m'appelle _____

C'est aujourd'hui _____

le _____

Comment allez-vous?

(How are you?)

I. Write a brief sentence of your own in French using the expression given. If you are not ready to do that, just copy the model sentence for practice.

16. **aller bien**   to be well   **Allez-vous bien aujourd'hui?**
Are you feeling well today?

_____

17. **aller mal**   not feel well   **Non, je vais toujours mal. Et vous?**
No, I'm still not feeling well. And you?

_____

18. **aller mieux**   to feel better   **Moi, je vais mieux aujourd'hui, merci.**
I'm feeling better today, thank you.

_____

19. **à la campagne**   to (in) the country   **Allez-vous à la campagne cette année?**
Are you going to the country this year?

_____

20. **passer une semaine**   to spend a week   **Oui, je vais passer une semaine à la campagne. Je pars demain.**
Yes, I'm going to spend one week in the country. I'm leaving tomorrow.

_____

II. On the line write in French one word that will make the sentence meaningful and grammatically correct.

1. **Allez-** _____ **bien aujourd'hui?**

2. **Non, je vais toujours** _____ **. Et vous?**

3. **Moi, je** _____ **mieux aujourd'hui, merci.**

4. **Allez-vous à** _____ **campagne cette année?**

5. **Oui, je vais** _____ **une semaine à la campagne.**

III. Answer the following questions in French in complete sentences.

1. **Comment allez-vous aujourd'hui?** _____

2. **Comment va votre ami(e)?** _____

3. **Que faites-vous quand vous êtes malade?** _____

_____

4. **Où allez-vous passer deux semaines cette année?** _____

_____

5. **Où allez-vous aujourd'hui?** _____

IV. List six words in French that you would use when talking about how you feel.

1. _____ 3. _____ 5. _____

2. _____ 4. _____ 6. _____

V. On the line write in French what the persons are doing.

La jeune fille et le garçon courent.

Que font-ils?
(What are they doing?)

Ils _____

VI. Write three adverbs in French that would describe how you feel.

1. _____ 2. _____ 3. _____

VII. A friend has asked you where you are going to spend one week this summer. On the line, write a complete sentence in French telling where you plan to go.

_____

VIII. A friend has asked you how many weeks you are going to spend in the country. On the line, write a complete sentence in French saying that you will spend either one week or two weeks.

_____

IX. Write three words in French naming things you would take with you when you spend two weeks in the country.

1. _____ 2. _____ 3. _____

X. Write a note to a friend saying that you are going to spend one week in the country and that you are leaving tomorrow. Begin your note with **Cher ami** (to a boy) or **Chère amie** (to a girl). End the note with **Amicalement** (In friendship). Then sign your name.

_____

_____

_____

XI. **Dialogue.** Write French words on the lines to complete the thought. It is a conversation between you and a doctor.

Le docteur: **Bonjour. Allez-vous** _____ **aujourd'hui?**

Vous: **Non, docteur. Je vais toujours** _____.

Le docteur: **Quel âge avez-vous?**

Vous: **J'ai** _____ **ans.**

Le docteur: **Prenez ce médicament** _____ **les matins.**

Vous: **Oui, docteur. Merci.**

J'ai faim et j'ai soif.

(I'm hungry and I'm thirsty.)

I.   Write a sentence of your own in French using the expression given. If you are not ready to do that, just copy the model sentence for practice.

21. **avoir envie de**   to feel like   **J'ai envie de manger.**
    (+ inf.)   (+ pres. part.)   I feel like eating.

    _____

22. **avoir faim**   to be hungry   **Je mange quand j'ai faim.**
                                                      I eat when I'm hungry.

    _____

23. **avoir soif**   to be thirsty   **Je bois quand j'ai soif.**
                                                      I drink when I'm thirsty.

    _____

24. **avoir l'habitude de**   to be in the habit of **J'ai l'habitude de manger chez moi.**
    (+ inf.)   (+ pres. part.)   I'm in the habit of eating at home.

    _____

25. **de temps à autre**   occasionally   **De temps à autre j'aime manger dans un**
                                                      restaurant.
                                                      Occasionally I like to eat in a restaurant.

    _____

II.   On the line write in French one word that will make the sentence meaningful and grammatically correct.

1. **J'** _____ **envie de manger.**

2. **Je mange quand j'ai** _____.

3. **Je bois quand j'ai** _____.

4. **J'** _____ **l'habitude de manger chez moi.**

5. **De temps à** _____ **j'aime manger dans un restaurant.**

III. Write French words to complete the paragraph. The words you need are in this lesson and in the previous ones.

J' _____ **faim et j'ai** _____. **Quand j'ai faim je** _____ **et quand j'ai**

soif je _____. **J'ai** _____ **de manger chez** _____ **mais aujourd'hui je**

vais _____ **dans un** _____.

IV. Look at the picture and study the statements in French. Then, on the lines, write answers in French to the questions.

1. **Qu'est-ce que c'est?**   2. **Est-ce un chapeau?**   3. **Non, ce n'est pas un chapeau.**
    (What is it?)   (Is it a hat?)   (No, it's not a hat.)
4. **C'est un gâteau.**   5. **Est-il délicieux?**   6. **Oui, il est délicieux.**
    (It's a cake.)   (Is it delicious?)   (Yes, it's delicious.)

Complete the answers in French.

1. **Qu'est-ce que c'est? Est-ce un chapeau?**

Non, *ce* _____. *C'est* _____.

2. **Est-il délicieux?** *Oui,* _____.

V. You are going to a supermarket. Write a short grocery list. Use French words in this lesson and in previous ones. You may also look up words in the vocabulary pages in the back of this book.

1. _____ 3. _____ 5. _____

2. _____ 4. _____ 6. _____

VI. Answer the following questions in French.

1. **Quand mangez-vous?** _____

2. **Quand buvez-vous?** _____

3. **Où avez-vous l'habitude de manger?** _____

_____

VII. A friend has invited you to dinner in a restaurant. You refuse politely and give one reason for not accepting the invitation. Write your response in French on the line.

_____

Je m'appelle _____

C'est aujourd'hui _____

le _____

Je vais au parc.
(I'm going to the park.)

I. Write a sentence of your own in French using the expression given. If you are not ready to do that, just copy the model sentence for practice.

26. **y a-t-il?**   is there? are there?   **Y a-t-il un parc dans cette ville?**
Is there a park in this city?

_____

27. **il y a**   there is, there are   **Oui, il y a deux parcs dans cette ville.**
Yes, there are two parks in this city.

_____

28. **près de**   near   **Il y a un parc près de ma maison.**
There is a park near my house.

_____

29. **jouer au tennis**   to play tennis   **Je joue au tennis dans le parc.**
I play tennis in the park.

_____

30. **jouer à la balle**   to play ball   **Je vais au parc maintenant pour jouer à la balle.**
I'm going to the park now to play ball.

_____

II. On the line write in French one word that will make the sentence meaningful and grammatically correct.

1. **Y a-t-** _____ **un parc dans cette ville?**

2. **Oui, il** _____ **a deux parcs dans cette ville.**

3. **Il y a un parc près** _____ **ma maison.**

4. **Je joue** _____ **tennis dans le parc.**

5. **Je vais au parc maintenant pour jouer** _____ **la balle.**

III. Write French words to complete the paragraph. The words you need are in this lesson.

    Il y a deux parcs dans cette ville. Il _____ **a un parc** _____ **de ma maison**

et il y _____ **un parc près de l'école. Je** _____ **au tennis dans le parc. Mainte-**

nant je _____ **au parc pour** _____ **à la balle.**

IV. Answer the following questions in French in complete sentences.

    1. **Combien de parcs y a-t-il dans votre ville?** _____

_____

    2. **Mentionnez trois choses qu'on trouve dans un parc.** _____

_____

    3. **Que faites-vous dans un parc?** _____

_____

    4. **Où jouez-vous au tennis?** _____

_____

    5. **Où allez-vous pour jouer à la balle?** _____

_____

V. On the lines write in French where the girl is and what she is doing.

**La jeune fille est
dans un parc.**

Elle joue à la balle.

Où est-elle?

Elle _____

Que fait-elle?

Elle _____

VI. A friend of yours asks you where you are going. Tell him or her that you are going to the park. You may give your own reason for going there or you may want to say that you are going to play ball or tennis. Write your response on the line.

_____

VII. **Dialogue.** You and a friend are talking about playing in the park. On the lines write French words to complete the thought. Use the vocabulary in this lesson or in the back pages of this book for words you do not know.

L'ami(e):   **Où vas-tu?**

Vous: **Je** _____ **au parc.**

L'ami(e):   **Pourquoi?**

Vous: **Pour** _____.

L'ami(e):   **Pour jouer à la balle?**

Vous: **Non, pour jouer** _____.

Je m'appelle _____

C'est aujourd'hui _____

le _____

I.   Write a short paragraph in French. Write that you are not feeling well today, that you are going to the country, and that you are going to spend two weeks in the country.

_____

_____

_____

_____

_____

_____

_____

II.   Write a short paragraph in French. Tell what you feel like doing now, what you do when you are hungry, what you do when you are thirsty, and where you are in the habit of eating.

_____

_____

_____

_____

_____

_____

_____

III.   Write a short paragraph in French. Tell how many parks there are in this city, if there is a park near your house, and two things that you do in a park.

_____

_____

_____

_____

_____

_____

_____

IV. Look at the pictures and answer the questions in French.

1.  **Que font-ils?**

   _____

2.  **Qu'est-ce que c'est?**

   _____

3.  **Que fait la jeune fille?**

   _____

proverbe **Il n'y a pas de fumée sans feu.**   Where there is smoke there is fire.

Je m'appelle _____

C'est aujourd'hui _____

le _____

Quelle heure est-il?
(What time is it?)

I. Write a sentence of your own in French using the expression given. If you are not ready to do that, just copy the model sentence for practice.

31. **Quelle heure est-il?**   What time is it?   **Quelle heure est-il?**
What time is it?

_____

32. **Il est une heure.**   It is one o'clock.   **Il est une heure. Non, je me trompe. Il est**
Il est deux heures.   It is two o'clock.   **deux heures.**
It is one o'clock. No, I'm mistaken. It is two o'clock.

_____

33. **à quelle heure . . .**   at what time . .   **A quelle heure allez-vous à la classe de français?**
At what time are you going to French class?

_____

34. **à trois heures**   at three o'clock   **Je vais à la classe de français à trois heures.**
I'm going to French class at three o'clock.

_____

35. **chez le dentiste**   at the dentist   **Moi, j'ai rendez-vous chez le dentiste à deux heures et demie.**
I have an appointment with the dentist at two thirty.

_____

II. On the line write in French one word that will make the sentence meaningful and grammatically correct.

1. **Quelle** _____ **est-il?**

2. **Il** _____ **une heure.**

3. **A** _____ **heure allez-vous à la classe de français?**

4. **Je vais à la classe de français à trois** _____.

5. **Moi, j'ai rendez-vous chez** _____ **dentiste à deux heures et demie.**

III. Answer the following questions in French.

1. **Quelle heure est-il?** _____

2. **A quelle heure prenez-vous le petit déjeuner?** _____

_____

3. **A quelle heure prenez-vous le déjeuner?** _____

_____

4. **A quelle heure prenez-vous le dîner?** _____

_____

5. **A quelle heure est-ce que vous vous couchez tous les soirs?** _____

_____

IV.   Write French words to complete the paragraph. The words you need are in this lesson. Read the paragraph at least one time before you write French words.

      Il est une _____. Non, je _____ trompe. Il est une heure _____

demie. Je _____ à la _____ de français à une heure et _____.

J' _____ rendez-vous _____ le dentiste à _____ heures et demie.

V.   On the lines under the clocks write in French the time that is given.

1.

2.

_____   _____

VI.   A friend of yours asks you at what time you are going to French class. Tell him or her that you are going to French class at three o'clock. Then tell your friend that you have an appointment with the dentist at four o'clock.

_____

_____

VII.   Write a list of places you have to go at a certain hour. For example, you are going to French class at one o'clock, you are going to the dentist at three o'clock, and you are going home at four o'clock. Or you may name other places and other times.

    1. _____

    2. _____

    3. _____

VIII.   You are working in a dentist's office. You answer a telephone call from Madame Durand. She would like you to take a message saying that she has an appointment with the dentist at three o'clock but she will be arriving at four o'clock. On the lines, write the phone message in French.

            La date _____

            L'heure _____

_____

_____

            Votre nom _____

Je m'appelle _____

C'est aujourd'hui _____

le _____

Voici un musée!   Voilà une bibliothèque!
(Here's a museum!)   (There's a library!)

I. Write a sentence of your own in French using the expression given. If you are not ready to do that, just copy the model sentence for practice.

36. **voici**   here is, here are   **Voici un musée!** Here is a museum!
                  (pointing out)   **On regarde des objets d'art dans un musée.**
                                            People look at *objets d'art* in a museum.

_____

37. **voilà**   there is, there are   **Voilà une bibliothèque!** There's a library!
                  (pointing out)   **On lit dans une bibliothèque.**
                                            People read in a library.

_____

38. **à droite** to (at) (on) the   **Voilà la gare à droite!** There's the station on the
                  right   right!
                                            On achète des billets dans une gare.
                                            People buy tickets in a station.

_____

39. **à gauche** to (at) (on) the left   **Voilà l'école à gauche!** There's the school on the
                                            left!
                                            On apprend à l'école. One learns at school.

_____

40. **il faut (+inf.)** it is necessary   **Il faut aller à droite pour trouver la gare.**
                         (+inf), one must   You must go to the right to find the station.

_____

II. On the line write in French one word that will make the sentence meaningful and grammatically correct.

1. **Voici** _____ **musée!**

2. **Voilà** _____ **bibliothèque!**

3. **Voilà la gare** _____ **droite!**

4. **Voilà l'école** _____ **gauche!**

5. **Il** _____ **aller à droite pour trouver la gare.**

III. Answer the following questions in French. You may write a complete sentence or only two or three words. Your answers must show that you understood the questions. What you write must be comprehensible.

1. **Qu'est-ce qu'on fait dans un musée?** _____

_____

2. **Qu'est-ce qu'on fait dans une bibliothèque?** _____

_____

3. **Qu'est-ce qu'on fait dans une école?** _____

_____

4. **Qu'est-ce qu'il faut faire pour apprendre?** _____

_____

5. **Où va-t-on pour prendre un train?** _____

_____

IV. On the lines write in French one activity that people do in the places indicated.

1. In a museum _____

2. In a library _____

3. In a train station _____

V. Here is a French train ticket. Examine it carefully. Answer the questions in French in just a few words.

```
┌─────────────────────────────────────────────────────────────┐
│  BILLET DE TRAIN                          Classe  2           │
│                                                               │
│  Départ      Rennes                                           │
│  Arrivée     Paris—Gare Montparnasse                          │
│  Utilisable  du 22 octobre au 21 décembre                     │
│                                                               │
│  Adultes  001   Animaux   000                   Prix    F148  │
│  Enfants  002   Réduction de prix  000   Numéro du billet  79748290005 │
└─────────────────────────────────────────────────────────────┘
```

1. **Quel est le prix du billet?** _____

2. **De quelle ville partez-vous?** _____

3. **A quelle ville allez-vous?** _____

4. **A quelle gare arrivez-vous?** _____

5. **En quelle classe voyagez-vous?** _____

6. **Le billet est pour combien d'adultes?** _____

_____

7. **Le billet est pour combien d'enfants?** _____

_____

8. **De quelle date à quelle date le billet est-il utilisable?** _____

_____

Je m'appelle _____

C'est aujourd'hui _____

le _____

Je lis, je réponds, je parle.

(I read, I answer, I talk.)

I. Write a sentence of your own in French using the expression given. If you are not ready to do that, just copy the model sentence for practice.

41. **au bas de**   at the bottom of   **Le devoir pour demain commence au bas de la page dix-huit.**
The assignment for tomorrow starts at the bottom of page eighteen.

_____

42. **en haut de**   at the top of   **Le devoir pour demain se termine en haut de la page vingt.**
The assignment for tomorrow ends at the top of page twenty.

_____

43. **à la page . . .**   on page . . .   **Je lis à la page quinze maintenant.**
I am reading on page fifteen now.

_____

44. **à haute voix**   in a loud voice, aloud   **Quelquefois je réponds au professeur à haute voix.**
Sometimes I answer the teacher in a loud voice.

_____

45. **à voix basse**   in a low voice, softly, in a soft voice   **Quelquefois je parle à voix basse.**
Sometimes I speak in a low voice.

_____

II. On the line write in French one word that will make the sentence meaningful and grammatically correct.

1. **Le devoir pour demain commence _____ bas de la page dix-huit.**

2. **Le devoir pour demain se termine _____ haut de la page vingt.**

3. **Je lis à _____ page quinze maintenant.**

4. **Quelquefois je réponds au professeur à _____ voix.**

5. **Quelquefois je parle à voix _____.**

III. Answer the following questions in French. You may write a complete sentence or only two or three words. Your answers must show that you understood the questions. What you write must be comprehensible.

1. **A quelle page commence le devoir pour demain?** _____

_____

2. **A quelle page se termine le devoir pour demain?** _____

_____

3. **A quelle page lisez-vous maintenant?** _____

_____

4. **Parlez-vous à haute voix ou à voix basse dans la classe de français?** _____

_____

5. **Que répondez-vous quand quelqu'un vous dit *Comment vous appelez-vous?*** _____

_____

IV. On the lines write in French an antonym (opposite meaning) for each of the following.

1. **au bas de** _____ 3. **commence** _____

2. **à haute voix** _____ 4. **à droite** _____

V. **Dialogue.** Write French words on the lines to complete the dialogue. It is a conversation between you and Robert about the French lesson for tomorrow.

Robert: **A quelle page commence le devoir pour demain?**

Vous: _____

Robert: **Et à quelle page se termine le devoir?**

Vous: _____

Robert: **A quelle page lis-tu maintenant?**

Vous: _____

Robert: **Est-ce que tu réponds au professeur à haute voix ou à voix basse?**

Vous: _____

VI. The following letters are scrambled. Place them in the correct order to form a French word. The words are all in this lesson.

1. **E A D M I N** _____ 4. **A E P G** _____

2. **R U P O** _____ 5. **E U N Q I Z** _____

3. **I G V N T** _____ 6. **R E O D V I** _____

VII.

Qu'est-ce que c'est?

C'est _____.

Je m'appelle _____

C'est aujourd'hui _____

le _____

I.   Write two sentences in French. Write that you are going to French class at one o'clock and that you have an appointment with the dentist at three thirty.

_____

_____

II.   Write a short paragraph in French containing four sentences. Tell what people do in a museum, in a library, in a railroad station, and in a school.

_____

_____

_____

_____

_____

_____

_____

III. Write a short paragraph in French containing three sentences. State on what page the assignment for tomorrow starts, on what page it ends, and on what page you are reading now.

_____

_____

_____

_____

_____

_____

IV.   Look at the pictures and answer the questions in French.

1. Qu'est-ce que c'est?

_____

2. **Quelle heure est-il?**

3. **Quelle heure est-il?**

BILLET DE TRAIN   Classe **2**

Départ   Lyon
Arrivée   Paris—Gare de Lyon
Utilisable   du 22 octobre au 21 décembre

| **Adultes** 002 | **Animaux** 000 | | **Prix** F176 |
| **Enfants** 001 | **Réduction de prix** 000 | **Numéro du billet** 79748290005 | |

4. **Quel est le prix du billet?** _____

_____

5. **De quelle ville partez-vous?** _____

_____

6. **A quelle ville allez-vous?** _____

_____

7. **A quelle gare arrivez-vous?** _____

_____

8. **En quelle classe voyagez-vous?** _____

_____

9. **Le billet est pour combien d'adultes?** _____

_____

10. **Le billet est pour combien d'enfants?** _____

_____

proverbe **Qui ne risque rien n'a rien.** Nothing ventured, nothing gained.

Write the heading in French as you have learned to do in the previous lessons.

_____

_____

J'écris une carte postale.
(I'm writing a post card.)

I. Write a sentence of your own in French using the expression given. If you are not ready to do that, just copy the model sentence for practice.

46. **se souvenir de**   to remember   **Cher Monsieur: Oui, je me souviens de vous.**
Dear Sir: Yes, I remember you.

_____

_____

47. **se rappeler**   to remember   **Je me rappelle l'incident dont vous parlez aussi.**
I remember the incident you are talking about also.

_____

_____

48. **avoir l'intention de (+ inf.)**   to intend, to plan   **J'ai l'intention de vous donner ma réponse bientôt.**
I intend to give you my answer soon.

_____

_____

49. **à cette heure**   at this moment   **Malheureusement, à cette heure je suis très occupé.**
Unfortunately, at this moment I am very busy.

_____

_____

50. **veuillez accepter . . .**   please accept . . .   **Veuillez accepter l'expression de mes meilleurs sentiments.**
Please accept my best wishes.

_____

_____

II. Write a post card in French to Monique Dupont, your French pen pal. Tell her at least three things about yourself. Refer to the previous lessons if you have to.

Chère Monique,

_____
_____
_____
_____
_____ .

Amicalement,

_____

Mlle Monique Dupont
15, rue des Fleurs
75014 Paris
France

PAR AVION

III. Answer the following questions in French. You may write a complete sentence or only two or three words. Your answers must show that you understood the questions. What you write must be comprehensible.

1. **Qu'est-ce que vous avez l'intention de faire cet après-midi?** _____
_____
_____

2. **Où est votre meilleur(e) ami(e) à cette heure?** _____
_____
_____

3. **Qu'est-ce que vous aimez faire chaque soir après le dîner?** _____
_____

4. **Nommez trois fruits que vous aimez.** _____
_____
_____

5. **Quel jour sommes-nous aujourd'hui?** _____
_____
_____

IV. Read the following business letter. Then answer the questions below it. You may write a complete sentence or only two or three words. Your answers must show that you understood the questions. What you write must be comprehensible. Don't forget to use the vocabulary pages in the back of this book.

Samedi, le 22 novembre

Monsieur Michel Dubois
Le Directeur
BICYCLETTES MODERNES
282, Avenue du Parc
75014 Paris

Cher Monsieur:

Envoyez-moi, s'il vous plaît, votre catalogue. Je voudrais acheter une bicyclette rouge pour participer au Tour de France.

Merci mille fois.

Veuillez accepter l'expression de mes meilleurs sentiments.

Jacqueline Pucelle
Jacqueline Pucelle
10, rue des Jardins
75006 Paris

1. **Quelle est la date de la lettre?** _____

_____

2. **Qui écrit la lettre?** _____

_____

3. **Qu'est-ce que Jacqueline Pucelle désire?** _____

_____

4. **Pourquoi désire-t-elle acheter une bicyclette rouge?** _____

_____

5. **Quelle est l'adresse de Jacqueline Pucelle?** _____

_____

Write the heading in French as you have learned to do in the previous lessons.

_____

_____

Ma maison
(My house)

I.   Write two sentences of your own in French using the expression given. If you are not ready to do that, just copy each model sentence twice for practice.

51. **demeurer**   to live, reside   **Je demeure dans une grande maison.**
                                                    I live in a big house.

                                                    _____

                                                    _____

52. **se trouver**   to be located   **Elle se trouve près d'ici.**
                                                    It is located near here.

                                                    _____

                                                    _____

53. **beaucoup de**   many, much   **Il y a beaucoup de fleurs dans notre jardin.**
                                                    There are many flowers in our garden.

                                                    _____

                                                    _____

54. **de temps en temps** from time to time   **De temps en temps je travaille dans le jardin.**
                                                    From time to time I work in the garden.

                                                    _____

                                                    _____

55. **à côté de**   beside, next to   **A côté de chez nous il y a de bons voisins.**
                                                    Next door to us there are good neighbors.

                                                    _____

                                                    _____

II.   On the line write in French one word that will make the sentence meaningful and grammatically correct.

1. **Je** _____ **dans une grande maison.**

2. **La maison se** _____ **près d'ici.**

3. **Il y a beaucoup** _____ **fleurs dans notre jardin.**

4. **De temps** _____ **temps je travaille dans le jardin.**

5. **A côté** _____ **chez nous il y a de bons voisins.**

III. Answer the following questions in French. You may write a complete sentence or only two or three words. Your answers must show that you understood the questions. What you write must be comprehensible.

1. **Où demeurez-vous?** _____

2. **Où se trouve votre maison?** _____

3. **Y a-t-il des fleurs dans votre jardin?** _____

_____

4. **Que faites-vous dans le jardin?** _____

_____

5. **Qui demeure à côté de chez vous?** _____

_____

IV. Read the following advertisement from a French newspaper. On the lines, write in French three things that sometimes need repair in your house—for example, a faucet, radiator, dryer, and so on. Or you may want to say in French the plumbing, heating, electricity.

1. _____ 2. _____ 3. _____

S. O. S. SERVICES
15, rue Jean-Jacques
75028 Paris
Tél. 43-44-25-37

●Plomberie   ●Chauffage

●Electricité

Service vite et excellent—24 heures de service
●jour et nuit●

V. Answer the following questions in French. Use the vocabulary pages in the back of this book if necessary.

Qu'est-ce que c'est?

Qu'est-ce que c'est?

1. _____   2. _____

Write the heading in French as you have learned to do in the previous lessons.

_____

_____

Je me lave et je m'habille.

(I wash myself and dress myself.)

I. Write two sentences of your own in French using the expression given. If you are not ready to do that, just copy each model sentence twice for practice.

56. **se laver** to get washed, to wash oneself **Je me lave tous les matins.** I wash myself every morning.

_____

_____

57. **avant de (+ inf.)** before (+ present participle) **Avant de quitter la maison, je me lave.** Before leaving the house, I wash myself.

_____

_____

58. **se brosser les dents** to brush one's teeth **Je me brosse les dents tous les matins.** I brush my teeth every morning.

_____

_____

59. **se brosser les cheveux** to brush one's hair **Je me brosse les cheveux tous les matins.** I brush my hair every morning.

_____

_____

60. **s'habiller** to get dressed, to dress oneself **Je m'habille dans ma chambre.** I get dressed in my room.

_____

_____

II. On the line write in French one word that will make the sentence meaningful and grammatically correct.

1. **Je me** _____ **tous les matins.**

2. **Avant** _____ **quitter la maison, je me lave.**

3. **Je me** _____ **les dents tous les matins.**

4. **Je** _____ **brosse les cheveux tous les matins.**

5. **Je m'** _____ **dans ma chambre.**

III. Answer the following questions in French. You may write a complete sentence or only two or three words. Your answers must show that you understood the questions. What you write must be comprehensible. Answers with just **oui** or **non** are not acceptable.

1. **Est-ce que vous vous lavez tous les matins?** _____

_____

2. **Est-ce que vous vous lavez avant de quitter la maison?** _____

_____

3. **Est-ce que vous vous brossez les dents tous les matins?** _____

_____

4. **Est-ce que vous vous brossez les cheveux?** _____

_____

5. **Où est-ce que vous vous habillez?** _____

_____

IV. **Lists.** In the spaces below, write a list of words in French as directed in each situation. They are all in this lesson.

A. Write three verbs in French that you would use to describe the picture.

1. _____ 2. _____ 3. _____

B. Write three nouns in French that you would use to describe the picture.

1. _____ 2. _____ 3. _____

Write the heading in French as you have learned to do in the previous lessons.

_____

_____

I. Write a post card in French to Monique Dupont, your French pen pal. Tell her at least three things about yourself.

II. Write four sentences in French. Tell what kind of house you live in (big or small), where it is located, something about flowers in the garden, and a word or two about the neighbors next door.

_____

_____

_____

_____

III. **Lists.** Write four words in French of things in your house that sometimes need to be repaired.

1. _____ 2. _____ 3. _____ 4. _____

IV. On the lines write the missing words in French. They are all in lessons 10, 11, 12.

1. **Je me souviens de** _____.

2. **à** _____ **heure?**

3. **Qu'est-ce** _____**?**

4. **Qui** _____ **la lettre?**

5. **Jacqueline** _____ **une bicyclette.**

6. **Je demeure dans une** _____ **maison.**

7. **Je** _____ **dans le jardin.**

8. **Je me** _____ **les cheveux.**

9. **Je m'habille dans ma** _____ **.**

10. **Je me lave tous les** _____ **.**

V.   **Dialogue.** Look at the picture below and complete the dialogue by writing one word in French on the lines.

La mère: **Joseph, tu ne te** _____ **pas.**
①

Le garçon: **Mais, maman, je** _____ **lave les mains tous les** _____ **.**
② ③

La mère: **Tu ne te** _____ **pas les cheveux.**
④

Le garçon: **Okay, maman. Je vais me laver et je vais me brosser les** _____ **.**
⑤

proverbe **Plus ça change, plus c'est la même chose.**
The more it changes, the more it remains the same.

Write the heading in French as you have learned to do in the previous lessons.

_____

_____

Je vais faire un voyage.
(I'm going to take a trip.)

I. Write two sentences of your own in French using the expression given. If you are not ready to do that, just copy each model sentence twice for practice.

61. **faire un voyage**   to take a trip, to go on a trip   **Je vais faire un voyage demain.**
I am going on a trip tomorrow.

_____

_____

62. **faire la malle**   to pack a trunk   **Il faut faire la malle tout de suite.**
I must pack a trunk right away.

_____

_____

63. **faire la valise**   to pack a suitcase   **Il faut faire les valises aussi.**
I must pack the suitcases, too.

_____

_____

64. **de bonne heure**   early   **Il faut me lever de bonne heure.**
I must get up early.

_____

_____

65. **se coucher**   to go to bed   **Il faut me coucher de bonne heure.**
I must go to bed early.

_____

_____

II. On the line write in French one word that will make the sentence meaningful and grammatically correct.

1. **Je vais** _____ **un voyage demain.**

2. **Il faut** _____ **la malle tout de suite.**

3. **Il** _____ **faire les valises aussi.**

4. **Il faut me lever de** _____ **heure.**

5. **Il faut me** _____ **de bonne heure.**

III. Answer the following questions in French. You may write a complete sentence or only two or three words. Your answers must show that you understood the questions. What you write must be comprehensible.

1. **Qu'est-ce que vous allez faire demain?** _____

_____

2. **Qu'est-ce qu'il faut faire tout de suite?** _____

_____

3. **Qu'est-ce qu'il faut faire aussi?** _____

_____

4. **Pourquoi est-ce qu'il faut vous lever de bonne heure?** _____

_____

5. **Pourquoi est-ce qu'il faut vous coucher de bonne heure?** _____

_____

IV.   **Qu'est-ce que c'est?**   **Et qu'est-ce que c'est?**

1. _C'est..._ _____   2. _C'est..._ _____

V.   **Lists.** In the spaces below, write a list of words in French as directed in each situation. They are all in this lesson.

A. Write two words in French naming things you will have to pack in preparing to take a trip.

1. _____ 2. _____

B. Write three expressions in French, each containing a verb, that you would use when talking about a trip you plan to take.

1. _____ 2. _____ 3. _____

VI. Write a short paragraph in French consisting of at least three sentences saying that you are going on a trip tomorrow, that you must pack a trunk right away, and that you must pack the suitcases, too.

_____

_____

_____

Write the heading in French as you have learned to do in the previous lessons.

_____

_____

J'ai chaud et j'ai de la fièvre.

(I feel warm and I have a fever.)

I. Write two sentences of your own in French using the expression given. If you are not ready to do that, just copy each model sentence twice for practice.

66. **avoir chaud** to be (feel) warm **J'ai chaud. Ouvrez la fenêtre, s'il vous plaît.**
I feel warm. Open the window, please.

_____

_____

67. **avoir froid** to be (feel) cold **Vous avez froid; puis vous avez chaud.**
You feel cold; then you feel warm.

_____

_____

68. **avoir sommeil** to be (feel) sleepy **J'ai sommeil aussi.**
I feel sleepy, too.

_____

_____

69. **avoir besoin de** to need, have need of **Vous avez besoin de repos. Je pense que vous avez de la fièvre.**
You need some rest. I think you have a fever.

_____

_____

70. **faire venir** to send for **Je vais faire venir le médecin.**
I'm going to send for the doctor.

_____

_____

II. On the line write in French one word that will make the sentence meaningful and grammatically correct.

1. **J'** _____ **chaud. Ouvrez la fenêtre, s'il vous plaît.**

2. **Vous** _____ **froid; puis vous avez chaud.**

3. **J'** _____ **sommeil aussi.**

4. **Vous** _____ **besoin de repos.**

5. **Je vais** _____ **venir le médecin.**

III. Answer the following questions in French. You may write a complete sentence or only two or three words. Your answers must show that you understood the questions. What you write must be comprehensible.

1. **Que faites-vous quand vous avez chaud?** _____

    _____

2. **Que faites-vous quand vous avez froid?** _____

    _____

3. **Que faites-vous quand vous avez sommeil?** _____

    _____

4. **De quoi avez-vous besoin quand il pleut?** _____

    _____

5. **Quel est votre premier repas du jour?** _____

    _____

IV. Look at the picture. Write French words and expressions you could use to describe the scene.

1. _____ 2. _____ 3. _____

4. _____ 5. _____ 6. _____

Write the heading in French as you have learned to do in the previous lessons.

_____

_____

Je fais une promenade.

(I'm taking a walk.)

I. Write two sentences of your own in French using the expression given. If you are not ready to do that, just copy each model sentence twice for practice.

71. **s'amuser**   to have a good time, to enjoy oneself   **Je m'amuse le samedi.**
I have a good time on Saturdays.

_____

_____

72. **faire une promenade**   to take a walk   **Je fais une promenade le samedi.**
I take a walk on Saturdays.

_____

_____

73. **faire une promenade en voiture**   to go for a drive   **Je fais une promenade en voiture tous les samedis.**
I go for a drive every Saturday.

_____

_____

74. **le long de**   along   **Je fais une promenade le long du fleuve.**
I take a walk along the river.

_____

_____

75. **jouer du violon**   to play the violin   **Je joue du violon tous les samedis matins. Je sais jouer du piano, aussi.**
I play the violin on Saturday mornings. I know how to play the piano, too.

_____

_____

II. On the line write in French one word that will make the sentence meaningful and grammatically correct.

1. **Je m'_____ le samedi.**

2. **Je _____ une promenade le samedi.**

3. **Je fais une promenade en _____ tous les samedis.**

4. Je fais une _____ le long du fleuve.

5. Je joue _____ violon.

III. Answer the following questions in French. You may write a complete sentence or only two or three words. Your answers must show that you understood the questions. What you write must be comprehensible.

   1. **Quel jour de la semaine est-ce que vous vous amusez?** _____

   _____

   2. **Où aimez-vous faire une promenade le samedi?** _____

   _____

   3. **Savez-vous jouer du violon?** _____

   _____

   4. **Mentionnez deux choses que vous faites pour vous amuser.** _____

   _____

   5. **Comment est-ce que vous vous amusez dans un parc?** _____

   _____

IV. On the lines write in French what each person is doing.

   Qu'est-ce qu'il fait?   **Qu'est-ce qu'elle fait?**

   1. _____   2. _____

V. Write a short paragraph in French stating at least five things that you do on Saturdays.

   _____

   _____

   _____

VI. How many French words can you find hidden in the word **PROMENADE?** Find at least four.

   | P R O M E N A D E |

   1. _____ 2. _____ 3. _____ 4. _____

VII. Change one letter in any part of the word and get another French word. The words are all in this lesson.

   Example: **bon** You write: _non_

   1. **je** _____   3. **jour** _____

   2. **vais** _____   4. **lait** _____

40   Je fais une promenade

Write the heading in French.

_____

_____

I.   Qu'est-ce que c'est?

1. _____

II.   Write a short paragraph in French consisting of at least three sentences saying that you are going on a trip tomorrow, that you must pack a trunk right away, and that you must pack the suitcases, too.

_____

_____

_____

_____

III.   Write a short paragraph in French consisting of at least three sentences describing a person who is sick in bed with a fever and a doctor at the bedside.

_____

_____

_____

_____

IV.   Answer the following questions in French. You may write a complete sentence or only two or three words. Your answers must show that you understood the questions. What you write must be comprehensible.

1. **Quel jour de la semaine est-ce que vous vous amusez?** _____

_____

2. **Qu'est-ce que vous allez faire demain?** _____

_____

3. **Que faites-vous quand vous avez sommeil?** _____

_____

V.   Write in French what each person is doing.

Qu'est-ce qu'il fait?   **Qu'est-ce qu'elle fait?**

1. _____   2. _____

VI.   **Lists.** In the spaces below, write a list of words in French as directed in each situation.

A. Name two things you will have to pack in preparing to take a trip.

1. _____   2. _____

B. Write three expressions, each containing a verb, that you would use when talking about a trip you plan to take.

1. _____   2. _____   3. _____

C. Write four words you would use when telling about what you do on Saturdays.

1. _____   2. _____   3. _____   4. _____

VII.   Change one letter in any part of the word and get another French word.

Example: **non** You write: *bon* _____

1. **fais** _____   3. **je** _____

2. **jour** _____   4. **vois** _____

VIII. On the line write in French one word that will make the sentence meaningful and grammatically correct.

1. **Je** _____ **faire un voyage demain.**

2. **J'**_____ **chaud et j'ai de la** _____ **.**

3. **Je fais une** _____ **le long du fleuve.**

proverbe   **Vouloir, c'est pouvoir.**   Where there's a will there's a way.

Write the heading in French.

_____

_____

Nous chantons et nous mangeons.

(We sing and we eat.)

I. Write two sentences of your own in French using the expression given. If you are not ready to do that, just copy each model sentence twice for practice.

76. **tous les vendredis**   every Friday   **Tous les vendredis nous chantons dans notre club.**
Every Friday we sing in our club.

_____

_____

77. **avoir lieu**   to take place   **Les réunions ont lieu tous les vendredis.**
The meetings take place every Friday.

_____

_____

78. **par exemple**   for example   **Nous faisons beaucoup de choses; par exemple, nous mangeons dans un restaurant français.**
We do many things; for example, we eat in a French restaurant.

_____

_____

79. **en ville**   downtown   **Nous allons en ville de temps en temps.**
We go downtown from time to time.

_____

_____

80. **de plus**   furthermore, besides, in addition   **De plus, nous voyons des films français.**
In addition, we see French movies.

_____

_____

II. On the line write in French one word that will make the sentence meaningful and grammatically correct.

1. **Nous** _____ **dans un restaurant français.**

2. **Nous** _____ **des films français.**

3. **Nous** _____ **en ville de temps en temps.**

III. **Lists.** In the spaces below, write a list of words in French as directed in each situation.

A. Look at this picture of the man eating. Write six words you would use to describe the scene.

L'appétit vient en mangeant.
Appetite comes while eating.

1. _____ 2. _____ 3. _____

4. _____ 5. _____ 6. _____

B. You are a member of a French Club. Write three words and expressions you would use when telling someone what the members do in the club.

1. _____ 2. _____ 3. _____

IV. Answer the following questions in French. You may write a complete sentence or only two or three words. Your answers must show that you understood the questions. What you write must be comprehensible.

1. **Qu'est-ce que vous faites dans votre club?** _____

_____

2. **Quel jour les réunions ont-elles lieu?** _____

_____

3. **Qu'est-ce que vous faites de temps en temps pour vous amuser dans votre club?** _____

_____

4. **Où mangez-vous de temps en temps?** _____

_____

5. **Quels films voyez-vous?** _____

_____

Write the heading in French.

_____

_____

Pourquoi avez-vous l'air triste?

(Why do you look sad?)

I. Write two sentences of your own in French using the expression given. If you are not ready to do that, just copy each model sentence twice for practice.

81. **Qu'est-ce que vous avez?**   What's the matter?   **Qu'est-ce que vous avez?**
What's the matter?

_____

_____

82. **avoir l'air (+ adj.)**   to look (+ adj.), seem   **Vous avez l'air triste.**
You look sad.

_____

_____

83. **avoir honte**   to be (feel) ashamed   **J'ai honte parce que je ne sais pas la réponse.**
I'm ashamed because I don't know the answer.

_____

_____

84. **avoir tort**   to be wrong   **Vous avez tort d'avoir honte.**
You're wrong to feel ashamed.

_____

_____

85. **Cela ne fait rien.**   It doesn't matter.   **Cela ne fait rien.**
It doesn't matter.

_____

_____

II. On the line write in French one word that will make the sentence meaningful and grammatically correct.

1. **Qu'est-ce** _____ **vous avez?**

2. **Vous** _____ **l'air triste.**

3. **J'** _____ **honte parce que je ne sais pas la réponse.**

4. **Vous** _____ **tort d'avoir honte.**

5. **Cela** _____ **fait rien.**

III. **Lists.** In the spaces below write a list of words in French as directed in each situation.

A. Look at this picture of the boy who looks sad because he broke a neighbor's window. Write six words and expressions you would use to describe the scene. Use the vocabulary in the back pages.

1. _____ 2. _____ 3. _____

4. _____ 5. _____ 6. _____

B. Write French words that are the opposites (antonyms) for each of the following. Use the vocabulary in the back pages.
   1. **la réponse** _____ 3. **quelque chose** _____

   2. **triste** _____ 4. **avoir tort** _____

IV. **Writing letters or notes.** Write a note to a friend saying thank you for the basketball you received for your birthday. Begin the note with **Cher ami** or **Chère amie.** End the note with **Amitiés** (Friendship). Write at least six words.

_____

_____

_____

_____

_____

Write the heading in French.

_____

_____

J'étudie le français.
(I'm studying French.)

I. Write two sentences of your own in French using the expression given. If you are not ready to do that, just copy each model sentence twice for practice.

86. **depuis (+ length of time)**   for (since) (+ length of time)   **J'étudie le français depuis deux ans.**
I have been studying French for two years.

_____

_____

87. **faire de mon mieux**   to do my best   **Je fais de mon mieux dans la classe de français.**
I do my best in French class.

_____

_____

88. **faire des progrès**   to make progress   **Je fais des progrès dans la classe de français.**
I am making progress in French class.

_____

_____

89. **poser des questions**   to ask questions   **Je pose des questions dans la classe de français.**
I ask questions in French class.

_____

_____

90. **continuer à (+ inf.)**   to continue to (+ inf.)   **Je vais continuer à étudier le français l'année prochaine.**
I'm going to continue to study French next year.

_____

_____

II. On the line write in French one word that will make the sentence meaningful and grammatically correct.

1. **J'étudie le français** _____ **deux ans.**

2. **Je fais** _____ **mon mieux dans la classe de français.**

3. **Je fais** _____ **progrès dans la classe de français.**

J'étudie le français   **47**

4. **Je** _____ **des questions dans la classe de français.**

5. **Je vais continuer** _____ **étudier le français l'année prochaine.**

III. Look at this picture of the French teacher at her desk in the classroom. List a few words or expressions in French that you would use to describe the scene.

le tableau
le globe
la chaise
la maîtresse de français
le bureau

1. _____ 2. _____ 3. _____

4. _____ 5. _____ 6. _____

IV. Answer the following questions in French. You may write a complete sentence or only two or three words. Your answers must show that you understood the questions. What you write must be comprehensible.

1. **Depuis combien de temps étudiez-vous le français?** _____

_____

2. **Allez-vous continuer à étudier le français l'année prochaine? Pourquoi?** _____

_____

3. **Mentionnez trois choses que vous faites dans la classe de français.** _____

_____

V. **Dialogue.** You are a tourist in Paris and are talking in French with a saleslady (**une vendeuse**) in a department store while you are paying for something you bought.

La vendeuse: **Où avez-vous appris à parler si bien le français?**

Vous: _____
(Tell her in school)

La vendeuse: **Depuis combien de temps?**

Vous: _____
(Tell her you have been studying French for two years.)

La vendeuse: **Allez-vous continuer à étudier la langue?**

Vous: _____
(Tell her you're going to continue to study French next year.)

La vendeuse: **Vous êtes extraordinaire!**

Vous: _____
(Thank her and say good-bye.)

Write the heading in French.

_____

_____

I. Look at this picture of the French teacher at her desk in the classroom. List a few words or expressions in French that you would use to describe the scene.

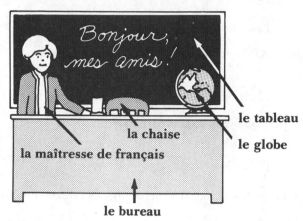

Bonjour, mes amis!

le tableau

la chaise

le globe

la maîtresse de français

le bureau

1. _____ 2. _____ 3. _____

4. _____ 5. _____ 6. _____

II. Answer the following questions in French. You may write a complete sentence or only two or three words. Your answers must show that you understood the questions. What you write must be comprehensible.

1. **Qu'est-ce que vous avez? Vous avez l'air triste.** _____

_____

2. **Quel est le contraire de l'expression** *avoir tort?* _____

_____

3. **Qu'est-ce que vous faites dans votre club?** _____

_____

4. **Quel jour les réunions de votre club ont-elles lieu?** _____

_____

5. **Quels films voyez-vous?** _____

_____

III. On the line write in French one word that will make the sentence meaningful and grammatically correct.

1. **Dans un restaurant français nous** _____.

2. **De temps en temps nous** _____ **en ville.**

3. **Nous** _____ **des films français.**

4. **J'étudie le français** _____ **deux ans.**

5. **Je fais des progrès dans la** _____ **de français.**

IV. **Dialogue.** You are a tourist in Paris and are talking in French with a saleslady (**une vendeuse**) in a department store while you are paying for something you bought.

La vendeuse: **Où avez-vous appris à parler si bien le français?**

Vous: _____

(Tell her in school)

La vendeuse: **Depuis combien de temps?**

Vous: _____

(Tell her you have been studying French for two years.)

La vendeuse: **Allez-vous continuer à étudier la langue?**

Vous: _____

(Tell her you're going to continue to study French next year.)

La vendeuse: **Vous êtes extraordinaire!**

Vous: _____

(Thank her and say good-bye.)

V. Write French words that are the opposites (antonyms) for each of the following.

1. **la réponse** _____   3. **quelque chose** _____

2. **triste** _____   4. **avoir tort** _____

proverbe   **Qui vivra verra.**   Time will tell.

Write the heading in French.

_____

_____

Je vais au cinéma.

(I'm going to the movies.)

I. Write two sentences of your own in French using the expression given. If you are not ready to do that, just copy each model sentence twice for practice.

91. **combien de** how many, how much

Combien de fois par mois allez-vous au cinéma?
How many times a month do you go to the movies?

_____

_____

92. **d'habitude** ordinarily, usually

D'habitude je vais au cinéma deux fois par mois.
Ordinarily I go to the movies twice a month.

_____

_____

93. **en face de** opposite

Le cinéma est en face de la bibliothèque.
The movie theater is opposite the library.

_____

_____

94. **faire plaisir** to please

Quand nous allons au cinéma, mon ami achète les billets. Cela me fait plaisir.
When we go to the movies, my friend buys the tickets. That pleases me.

_____

_____

95. **à l'heure** on time

Nous arrivons toujours à l'heure au cinéma.
We always arrive at the movies on time.

_____

_____

II. On the line write in French one word that will make the sentence meaningful and grammatically correct.

1. **Combien** _____ **fois par mois allez-vous au cinéma?**

2. **D'**_____ **je vais au cinéma deux fois par mois.**

3. **Le cinéma est en** _____ **de la bibliothèque.**

4. **Cela me** _____ **plaisir.**

5. **Nous arrivons toujours à l'** _____ **au cinéma.**

III. In the boxes, write the letters of the French words for the English words next to the numbers. They are all in this lesson. They all cross with the word **cinéma.**

1. to buy

2. ticket

3. my (*masc., sing.*)

4. movies

5. month

6. friend (*masc., sing.*)

IV. Answer the following questions in French in only two or three words, maybe even four. You do not have to write a complete sentence with a subject and verb. Your answers must show that you understood the questions. What you write must be comprehensible.

1. **Combien de fois par mois allez-vous au cinéma?** _____

_____

2. **D'habitude, avec qui allez-vous au cinéma?** _____

_____

3. **Où est le cinéma?** _____

_____

4. **Qui achète les billets?** _____

_____

5. **En général, est-ce que vous arrivez au cinéma de bonne heure, à l'heure, ou en retard?**

_____

V. **Dialogue.** You just met a friend downtown and you are on your way to the movies. Complete the dialogue using a few words in French.

Robert: **Où vas-tu?**

Toi: _____
(Tell him you're going to the movies.)

Robert: **Où est le cinéma?**

Toi: _____
(Tell him it's opposite the library.)

Robert: **Vas-tu souvent au cinéma?**

Toi: _____
(Tell him you go to the movies twice a month.)

Write the heading in French.

_____

_____

DEVOIR

20

Paul ne parle à personne.

(Paul doesn't speak to anyone.)

I. Write two sentences of your own in French using the expression given. If you are not ready to do that, just copy each model sentence twice for practice.

96. **ne . . . personne**   nobody, no one, not anyone   **Paul ne parle à personne.**
Paul doesn't speak to anyone. *Or:* Paul speaks to no one.

_____

_____

97. **ne . . . aucun**   no, not any   **Il n'a aucun ami.**
He hasn't any friends. *Or:* He has no friends.

_____

_____

98. **ne . . . plus**   no longer, not any more   **Il ne vient plus chez nous.**
He doesn't come to our house any more. *Or:* He no longer comes to our house.

_____

_____

99. **ne . . . rien**   nothing, not anything   **Il ne me dit rien.**
He doesn't say anything to me. *Or:* He says nothing to me.

_____

_____

100. **ne . . . jamais**   never   **Je ne lui parlerai jamais!**
I will never speak to him!

_____

_____

II. On the line write in French one word that will make the sentence meaningful and grammatically correct.

1. **Paul** _____ **parle à personne.**

2. **Il n'a** _____ **ami.**

3. **Il** _____ **vient plus chez nous.**

4. **Il ne me dit** _____ .

5. **Je** _____ **lui parlerai jamais!**

III. Answer the following questions in French *in the negative*. You do not have to write a complete sentence with a subject or verb. Just two or three words, maybe even four, are enough. Answering with just **non** is not acceptable. Your answers must show that you understood the questions. What you write must be comprehensible.

1. **Voyez-vous quelqu'un?** _____

2. **Avez-vous des frères?** _____

3. **Voyez-vous quelque chose?** _____

4. **Avez-vous été en Chine?** _____

IV. Write the letters of the French words for the English words.

Verticalement
1. never

Horizontalement
2. nothing
3. nobody (no one)

V. Write the French words that are antonyms (opposite in meaning). Don't forget to use the vocabulary pages in the back of this book if necessary.

1. **quelque chose** _____   3. **toujours** _____

2. **quelqu'un** _____   4. **rien** _____

VI. Write five short sentences in French using the negations as indicated.

1. **ne . . . personne** _____

2. **ne . . . aucun** _____

3. **ne . . . plus** _____

4. **ne . . . rien** _____

5. **ne . . . jamais** _____

Write the heading in French.

_____

_____

Je commence à écrire en français.

(I'm beginning to write in French.)

I. Write two sentences of your own in French using the expression given. If you are still not ready to do that, just copy each model sentence twice for practice.

101. **être temps de**   to be time to   **Il est temps d'aller à la classe de français.**
It is time to go to French class.

_____

_____

102. **faire attention**   to pay attention   **Il faut faire attention en classe pour apprendre.**
You must pay attention in class in order to learn.

_____

_____

103. **commencer à (+ inf.)**   to begin (+ inf.)   **Cette année nous commençons à écrire en français.**
This year we are beginning to write in French.

_____

_____

104. **se servir de**   to use, make use of   **Pour écrire, je me sers d'un stylo et de papier.**
In order to write I use pen and paper.

_____

_____

105. **avoir de la chance**   to be lucky   **J'ai un excellent professeur de français. J'ai de la chance.**
I have an excellent French teacher. I'm lucky.

_____

_____

_____

II. On the line write in French one word that will make the sentence meaningful and grammatically correct.

1. Il est _____ d'aller à la classe de français.

2. Il faut _____ attention en classe pour apprendre.

3. Cette année nous commençons _____ écrire en français.

4. Pour écrire, je me _____ d'un stylo.

5. J'ai un excellent professeur de français. J'ai de _____ chance.

III. Answer the following questions in French. You do not have to write a complete sentence with a subject and verb. Just two or three words, maybe even four, are enough. Your answers must show that you understood the questions. What you write must be comprehensible.

1. **Que faut-il faire en classe pour apprendre?** _____

_____

2. **Qu'est-ce que vous commencez à faire cette année dans la classe de français?** _____

_____

3. **De quoi est-ce que vous vous servez pour écrire?** _____

_____

IV. **Que fait la femme?**
(What is the woman doing?)

Elle _____

V. After reading the following advertisement from a French newspaper, answer the questions in French using a few words.

PAPETERIE ROYALE

☐ papier   ☐ stylos
  ☐ cahiers   ☐ crayons
    ☐ règles   ☐ gommes

129, Avenue Royale, 75014 Paris
Tél. 43-92-66-29   **prix bas**

1. **Quel est le nom de cette papeterie?** _____

_____

2. **Quelle est l'adresse?** _____

_____

3. **Quel est le numéro de téléphone?** _____

_____

4. **Comment sont les prix?** _____

_____

5. **Que voulez-vous acheter dans cette papeterie?** _____

_____

Write the heading in French.

_____

_____

I. Write a short paragraph in French consisting of three sentences about going to the movies.

_____

_____

_____

_____

II. In the boxes, print the letters of the French words for the English words next to the numbers. They are all in this lesson. They all cross with the word **cinéma.**

1. to buy

2. ticket

3. my *(masc., sing.)*

4. movies

5. month

6. friend *(masc., sing.)*

III. **Dialogue.** You just met a friend downtown and you are on your way to the movies. Complete the dialogue using a few words in French.

Robert: **Où vas-tu?**

Toi: _____
(Tell him you're going to the movies.)

Robert: **Où est le cinéma?**

Toi: _____
(Tell him it's opposite the library.)

Robert: **Vas-tu souvent au cinéma?**

Toi: _____
(Tell him you go to the movies twice a month.)

IV. Write five short sentences in French using the negations as indicated.

1. **ne . . . personne** _____

2. **ne . . . aucun** _____

3. **ne . . . plus** _____

4. **ne . . . rien** _____

5. **ne . . . jamais** _____

V. **Que fait la femme?**

Elle _____

VI. After reading the following advertisement from a French newspaper, answer the questions in French using a few words.

PAPETERIE ROYALE

☐ papier   ☐ stylos
☐ cahiers   ☐ crayons
☐ règles   ☐ gommes

129, Avenue Royale, 75014 Paris
Tél. 43-92-66-29   **prix bas**

1. **Quel est le nom de cette papeterie?** _____

_____

2. **Quelle est l'adresse?** _____

_____

3. **Quel est le numéro de téléphone?** _____

_____

4. **Comment sont les prix?** _____

_____

5. **Que voulez-vous acheter dans cette papeterie?** _____

_____

proverbe   **L'air ne fait pas la chanson.** ⎫
            L'habit ne fait pas le moine. ⎭ Clothes don't make the person.

Write the heading in French.

_____

_____

Mon père vient de quitter la maison.
(My father has just left the house.)

I. Write two sentences of your own in French using the expression given. If you are still not ready to do that, just copy each model sentence twice for practice.

106. **venir de**   to have just   **Mon père vient de quitter la maison.**
     (+ infinitive)   (+ past participle)   My father has just left the house.

     _____

     _____

107. **rendre visite à**   to visit   **Il va rendre visite à mon oncle.**
                                                 He is going to visit my uncle.

     _____

     _____

108. **ressembler à**   to resemble,   **Mon père ressemble à mon oncle.**
                           look like   My father looks like my uncle.

     _____

     _____

109. **vouloir bien**   to be willing   **Je veux bien y aller avec lui.**
                                                 I am willing to go there with him.

     _____

     _____

110. **au lieu de**   instead of (+ pres-   **Au lieu de rester à la maison, je veux bien**
     (+ infinitive)   ent participle)   **l'accompagner.**
                                                 Instead of staying home, I am willing to
                                                 accompany him.

     _____

     _____

II. On the line write in French one word that will make the sentence meaningful and grammatically correct.

1. **Mon père vient _____ quitter la maison.**

2. **Il va _____ visite à mon oncle.**

3. **Mon père ressemble _____ mon oncle.**

4. **Je _____ bien y aller avec lui.**

5. **Au _____ de rester à la maison, je veux bien l'accompagner.**

III. Answer the following questions in French. You do not have to write a complete sentence with a subject and verb. Just two or three words, maybe even four, are enough. Your answers must show that you understood the questions. What you write must be comprehensible. Merely answering **oui** or **non** is not acceptable.

1. **Qui vient de quitter la maison?** _____

_____

2. **Où va-t-il (elle)?** _____

_____

3. **A qui est-ce que votre père ressemble?** _____

_____

4. **Voulez-vous bien aller avec votre père?** _____

_____

5. **Allez-vous rester à la maison?** _____

_____

IV. In French write a note to your cousin telling him or her that (a) your father has just left the house, (b) he is going to visit your uncle, and (c) instead of staying home you are willing to go there with him. Start the note with **Cher cousin** or **Chère cousine.** Close the note with **Bien à toi** and your name. Also, write the date in French.

_____

_____

_____

_____

_____

                                           _____

                                             _____

V. Print the missing letters for the following French verbs used in this lesson.

1. **V __ N __ R**   4. **R E __ S __ M B __ E R**

2. **V __ U L __ I R**   5. **R __ N D __ E**

3. **R __ S T __ R**   6. **A __ L __ R**

VI. How many French words can you find hidden in the word **MAISON?** Find at least six.

M A I S O N

1. _____   2. _____   3. _____

4. _____   5. _____   6. _____

Write the heading in French.

_____

_____

J'ai vu un clown au milieu de la rue.

(I saw a clown in the middle of the street.)

I. Write two sentences of your own in French using the expression given. If you are still not ready to do that, just copy each model sentence twice for practice.

111. **quelque chose de (+ adjectif)** — something (+ adjective) — **Hier j'ai vu quelque chose d'amusant.**
Yesterday I saw something funny.

_____

_____

112. **au milieu de** — in the middle of — **J'ai vu un clown au milieu de la rue.**
I saw a clown in the middle of the street.

_____

_____

113. **de quelle couleur . . .** — what color . . . — **De quelle couleur était son costume? Il était jaune.**
What color was his costume? It was yellow.

_____

_____

114. **à la main** — in his hand — **Il tenait un singe à la main.**
He was holding a monkey in his hand.

_____

_____

115. **éclater de rire** — to burst out laughing — **J'ai éclaté de rire.**
I burst out laughing.

_____

_____

II. On the line write in French one word that will make the sentence meaningful and grammatically correct.

1. **Hier j'ai vu _____ chose d'amusant.**

2. **J'ai vu un clown au _____ de la rue.**

3. **De _____ couleur était son costume?**

4. **Il tenait un singe _____ la main.**

5. **J'ai éclaté _____ rire.**

III. Answer the following questions in French. You do not have to write a complete sentence with a subject and verb. Just two or three words, maybe even four, are enough. Your answers must show that you understood the questions. What you write must be comprehensible.

1. **Qu'est-ce que vous avez vu hier?** _____

_____

2. **Où l'avez-vous vu?** _____

_____

3. **Qu'est-ce que vous avez fait?** _____

_____

4. **De quelle couleur était le costume du clown?** _____

_____

5. **De quelle couleur sont vos chaussures?** _____

_____

IV. Write three short sentences in French about something funny you saw yesterday. Tell (a) what you saw, (b) where you saw it, and (c) what you did.

1. _____

2. _____

3. _____

V.

Qu'est-ce que le petit garçon tient à la main?

Votre réponse: _____

VI. **Une devinette** (a riddle). **Qu'est-ce qu'il y a au milieu de Paris?**

Votre réponse: _____

VII. **Friendly persuasion.** Your friend is making plans to go with you to see the clowns and monkeys at a circus which is in town. You prefer to go to the movies. Write four words or expressions in French that you would use to persuade your friend to go to the movies instead of the circus.

1. _____   2. _____

3. _____   4. _____

Write the heading in French.

_____

_____

A qui est ce stylo?

(Whose is this pen?)

I. Write two sentences of your own in French using the expression given.

116. **être à**   to belong to   **A qui est ce stylo? Ce stylo est à moi.**
Whose pen is this? This pen is mine.

_____

_____

117. **bon marché**   cheap, inexpensive,   **Je l'ai acheté bon marché.**
at a bargain   I paid very little for it. _Or:_ I bought it for very little.

_____

_____

118. **là-bas**   over there   **La boutique se trouve là-bas.**
The shop is located over there.

_____

_____

119. **de l'autre côté**   on the other side   **La boutique se trouve de l'autre côté de la rue.**
The shop is located on the other side of the street.

_____

_____

120. **de bon coeur**   willingly   **Je ne l'ai pas payé cher et j'ai payé de bon coeur.**
I did not pay much for it and I paid willingly.

_____

_____

II. On the line write in French one word that will make the sentence meaningful and grammatically correct.

1. **A qui** _____ **ce stylo?**

2. **Je l'ai acheté** _____ **marché.**

3. **La boutique se** _____ **là-bas.**

4. **Je ne l'ai pas payé** _____ **.**

III. Answer the questions in French either in complete sentences with a subject and verb or in just a few words.

1. **Qu'est-ce que c'est?**

   _____

2. **Où l'avez-vous acheté?**

   _____

3. **Où se trouve la boutique?**

   _____

4. **Avez-vous payé cher?**

   _____

IV. Write a short paragraph in French containing at least three sentences. Write about something you bought stating its color, where you bought it, where the shop is located, and if you paid a lot or very little for it.

_____

_____

_____

_____

_____

_____

V. **Providing/obtaining information.** You are in a stationery shop **(une papeterie)** because you want to buy a pen. You are trying to obtain information from the clerk. The clerk is providing you with the information you are asking for. Write in French four words and expressions you and the clerk would use during the conversation.

1. _____   3. _____

2. _____   4. _____

VI. Write four verbs in French used in this lesson.

1. _____   3. _____

2. _____   4. _____

VII. Write four idiomatic expressions in French used in this lesson.

1. _____   3. _____

2. _____   4. _____

VIII. Change one letter in any part of the word and get another French word. The word you get is used in this lesson.

1. **soeur** (sister) _____ (heart) 2. **que** (what) _____ (who)

Write the heading in French.

_____

_____

I. Answer the following questions in French. You do not have to write a complete sentence with a subject and verb. Just two or three words, maybe even four, are enough. Your answers must show that you understood the questions. What you write must be comprehensible. Merely answering **oui** or **non** is not acceptable.

1. **Qui vient de quitter la maison?** _____

_____

2. **Où va-t-il (elle)?** _____

_____

3. **A qui est-ce que votre père ressemble?** _____

_____

4. **Voulez-vous bien aller avec votre père?** _____

_____

5. **Allez-vous rester à la maison?** _____

_____

II. In French write a note to your cousin telling him or her that (a) your father has just left the house, (b) he is going to visit your uncle, and (c) instead of staying home you are willing to go there with him. Start the note with **Cher cousin** or **Chère cousine.** Close the note with **Bien à toi** and your name. Also, write the date in French.

_____

_____

_____

_____

_____

_____

_____

_____

_____

III. Write three short sentences in French about something funny you saw yesterday. Tell (a) what you saw, (b) where you saw it, and (c) what you did.

1. _____

2. _____

3. _____

IV.

Qu'est-ce que le petit garçon tient à la main?

Votre réponse: _____

V. **Une devinette** (a riddle). **Qu'est-ce qu'il y a au milieu de Paris?**

Votre réponse: _____

VI. **Friendly persuasion.** Your friend is making plans to go with you to see the clowns and monkeys at a circus which is in town. You prefer to go to the movies. Write four words or expressions in French that you would use to persuade your friend to go to the movies instead of the circus.

1. _____ 2. _____

3. _____ 4. _____

VII. Answer the questions in French either in complete sentences with a subject and verb or in just a few words.

1. **Qu'est-ce que c'est?**   3. **Où se trouve la boutique?**

_____   _____

2. **Où l'avez-vous acheté?**   4. **Avez-vous payé cher?**

_____   _____

VIII. **Providing/obtaining information.** You are in a stationery shop **(une papeterie)** because you want to buy a pen. You are trying to obtain information from the clerk. The clerk is providing you with the information you are asking for. Write in French four words and expressions you and the clerk would use during the conversation.

1. _____ 3. _____

2. _____ 4. _____

proverbe **Beaucoup de bruit pour rien.**   Much ado about nothing.

Write the heading in French.

DEVOIR

25

Je suis allé(e) chez le médecin.

(I went to the doctor.)

I. Write two sentences of your own in French using the expression given.

121. **la semaine dernière**   last week   **La semaine dernière je suis allé(e) chez le médecin.**
Last week I went to the doctor.

_____

_____

122. **se faire mal**   to hurt oneself   **Je m'étais fait mal.**
I had hurt myself.

_____

_____

123. **se casser**   to break   **Je me suis cassé un doigt.**
I broke a finger.

_____

_____

124. **à peine**   hardly, scarcely   **Maintenant je peux à peine écrire.**
Now I can hardly write.

_____

_____

125. **ne pas (+ inf.)**   not to (+ inf.)   **Le médecin m'a dit de ne pas écrire.**
The doctor told me not to write.

_____

_____

II. On the line write in French one word that will make the sentence meaningful and grammatically correct.

1. **La semaine** _____ **je suis allé(e) chez le médecin.**

2. **Je m'étais** _____ **mal.**

3. **Je me** _____ **cassé un doigt.**

4. **Maintenant je peux à** _____ **écrire.**

5. **Le médecin m'a dit de ne** _____ **écrire.**

Je suis allé(e) chez le médecin   **67**

III.   Write four French verbs used in this lesson.

1. _____   3. _____

2. _____   4. _____

IV.   Write two French idiomatic expressions used in this lesson.

1. _____   2. _____

V.   Read the following short paragraph once for general comprehension. Then read it a second time. On the line next to the number, write a French word to complete the thought.

La ____①____ dernière, je ____②____ allé(e) chez le médecin. Je m'étais ____③____ mal. Je me suis ____④____ un doigt. Maintenant, je ____⑤____ à peine écrire. Le ____⑥____ m'a dit ____⑦____ ne ____⑧____ écrire.

1. _____   5. _____

2. _____   6. _____

3. _____   7. _____

4. _____   8. _____

VI.   **Expressing personal feelings.** You are in the hospital because you broke a leg and an arm. A friend comes to visit you. Write four French words and expressions you would use during a conversation about how you feel.

1. _____   3. _____

2. _____   4. _____

VII.   Write a note to a friend saying that (a) last week you broke a finger, (b) you can hardly write, and (c) you went to see a doctor. Also say that the doctor told you not to write. Begin the note with **Cher ami** or **Chère amie** (Dear friend) and end the note with **à bientôt** (see you soon). Then write your name. Don't forget to write the date in French!

_____

_____

_____

_____

_____

_____

_____

_____

_____

_____

Write the heading in French.

_____

_____

Hier j'ai assisté à un mariage.

(Yesterday I attended a wedding.)

I.   Write·two sentences of your own in French using the expression given.

126. **assister à**   to attend,   **Hier j'ai assisté à un mariage.**
                       be present at   Yesterday I attended a wedding.

_____

_____

127. **en retard**   late   **J'y suis arrivé(e) en retard.**
                            I arrived there late.

_____

_____

128. **il y avait**   there were,   **Il y avait cent personnes.**
                      there was   There were one hundred people.

_____

_____

129. **à la fin**   at the end   **A la fin de la cérémonie, nous sommes allés dîner.**
                                 At the end of the ceremony, we went to have dinner.

_____

_____

130. **de bon appétit**   with good appetite   **J'ai mangé de bon appétit.**
                                               I ate with good appetite. *Or:* I ate heartily.

_____

_____

II.   On the line write in French one word that will make the sentence meaningful and grammatically correct.

1. **Hier j'** _____ **assisté à un mariage.**

2. **J'y suis arrivé(e)** _____ **retard.**

3. **Il** _____ **avait cent personnes.**

4. **A la** _____ **de la cérémonie, nous sommes allés dîner.**

5. **J'ai mangé** _____ **bon appétit.**

III. Answer the following questions in French. You do not have to write a complete sentence with a subject and verb. Just two or three words, maybe even four, are enough. Your answers must show that you understood the questions. What you write must be comprehensible. Merely answering **oui** or **non** is not acceptable.

1. **Avez-vous assisté à un mariage hier?** _____

_____

2. **Est-ce que vous êtes arrivé(e) à l'heure à la cérémonie?** _____

_____

3. **Combien de personnes y avait-il?** _____

_____

4. **Où êtes-vous allé(e) à la fin de la cérémonie?** _____

_____

5. **Comment avez-vous mangé?** _____

_____

IV. Write the past participle in French for each of the following verbs used in this lesson. Consult the vocabulary in the back pages if necessary.

1. **assister** _____   3. **arriver** _____

2. **aller** _____   4. **manger** _____

V. **Word Order.** The following words are scrambled. Write them in the correct order to form a sentence that is meaningful and grammatically correct.

1. **mariage / un / à / assisté / j'ai / hier**

_____

2. **personnes / cent / avait / y / il**

_____

VI. **Lists.** You have been invited to a wedding. You are planning to give the bride and groom a present. Write a list of four things in French that you are considering. Perhaps the articles shown below appeal to you.

1. _____   3. _____

2. _____   4. _____

Write the heading in French.

_____

_____

J'ai peur de traverser le parc la nuit.

(I'm afraid to cross the park at night.)

I. Write two sentences of your own in French using the expression given.

131. **afin de (+ inf.)**   in order to (+ inf.)   **Afin d'arriver chez moi, il faut traverser le parc.**
In order to get home, I must cross the park.

_____

_____

132. **avoir peur**   to be afraid   **J'ai peur de traverser le parc la nuit.**
I'm afraid to cross the park at night.

_____

_____

133. **par là**   that way, through there   **Je n'aime pas aller par là la nuit.**
I don't like going that way at night.

_____

_____

134. **avoir raison**   to be right   **J'ai raison d'avoir peur.**
I'm right to be afraid.

_____

_____

135. **bien entendu**   of course   **Bien entendu. C'est bien dangereux.**
Of course. It's quite dangerous.

_____

_____

II. On the line write in French one word that will make the sentence meaningful and grammatically correct.

1. **Afin d'arriver chez moi, il** _____ **traverser le parc.**

2. **J'**_____ **peur de traverser le parc la nuit.**

3. **Je n'aime pas aller** _____ **là la nuit.**

4. **J'**_____ **raison d'avoir peur.**

5. **Bien** _____ **. C'est bien dangereux.**

III. Look at the picture below. Write four French words or expressions you would use to describe the scene.

1. _____ 3. _____

2. _____ 4. _____

IV. Write four French idiomatic expressions that contain the verb **avoir.**

1. _____ 3. _____

2. _____ 4. _____

V. **Dialogue.** You and a friend are talking on the phone about meeting late at night. Complete the dialogue in French according to the directions.

Jacqueline: **Allô! C'est moi. Jacqueline.**

Toi: _____
(Respond by asking how she is. Then ask what she wants.)

Jacqueline: **Très bien. Ecoute. Veux-tu aller au cinéma avec moi ce soir à dix heures?**

Toi: _____
(Ask her which cinema.)

Jacqueline: **Le cinéma qui se trouve de l'autre côté du parc.**

Toi: _____
(Tell her no. You are afraid to cross the park at night.)

Jacqueline: **Oui. Tu as raison.**

Toi: _____
(Tell her it's quite dangerous. Suggest next Saturday afternnoon.)

Jacqueline: **D'accord. Okay. Au revoir.**

Toi: _____
(Tell her okay, then say good-bye.)

Write the heading in French.

_____

_____

I. Read the following short paragraph once for general comprehension. Then read it a second time. On the line next to the number, write a French word to complete the thought.

La ____①____ dernière, je ____②____ allé(e) chez le médecin. Je m'étais ____③____ mal. Je me suis ____④____ un doigt. Maintenant, je ____⑤____ à peine écrire. Le ____⑥____ m'a dit ____⑦____ ne ____⑧____ écrire.

1. _____ 5. _____

2. _____ 6. _____

3. _____ 7. _____

4. _____ 8. _____

II. **Expressing personal feelings.** You are in the hospital because you broke a leg and an arm. A friend comes to visit you. Write four French words and expressions you would use during a conversation about how you feel.

1. _____ 3. _____

2. _____ 4. _____

III. Write a note to a friend saying that (a) last week you broke a finger, (b) you can hardly write, and (c) you went to see a doctor. Also say that the doctor told you not to write. Begin the note with **Cher ami** or **Chère amie** (Dear friend) and end the note with **à bientôt** (see you soon). Then write your name. Don't forget to write the date in French!

_____

_____

_____

_____

_____

_____

_____

_____

IV. Look at the picture below. Write four French words or expressions you would use to describe the scene.

1. _____   3. _____

2. _____   4. _____

V. **Dialogue.** You and a friend are talking on the phone about meeting late at night. Complete the dialogue in French according to the directions.

Jacqueline: **Allô! C'est moi. Jacqueline.**

Toi: _____
(Respond by asking how she is. Then ask what she wants.)

Jacqueline: **Très bien. Ecoute. Veux-tu aller au cinéma avec moi ce soir à dix heures?**

Toi: _____
(Ask her which cinema.)

Jacqueline: **Le cinéma qui se trouve de l'autre côté du parc.**

Toi: _____
(Tell her no. You are afraid to cross the park at night.)

Jacqueline: **Oui. Tu as raison.**

Toi: _____
(Tell her it's quite dangerous. Suggest next Saturday afternoon.)

Jacqueline: **D'accord. Okay. Au revoir.**

Toi: _____
(Tell her okay, then say good-bye.)

proverbe **C'est en forgeant qu'on devient forgeron.**   Practice makes perfect.

Write the heading in French.

_____

_____

Je travaille de plus en plus.

(I am working more and more.)

I. Write two sentences of your own in French using the expression given.

136. **de plus en plus**   more and more   **Je travaille de plus en plus.**
I am working more and more.

_____

_____

137. **du matin au soir**   from morning until night   **Samedi j'ai travaillé du matin au soir.**
On Saturday I worked from morning until night.

_____

_____

138. **n'en pouvoir plus**   to be completely exhausted, not to be able to go on   **Je n'en pouvais plus. J'étais très fatigué(e).**
I couldn't go on. I was very tired.

_____

_____

139. **se reposer**   to rest   **Dimanche je me suis reposé(e).**
On Sunday I rested.

_____

_____

140. **se porter mieux**   to be (feel) better   **Aujourd'hui je me porte beaucoup mieux.**
Today I am feeling much better.

_____

_____

II. On the line write in French one word that will make the sentence meaningful and grammatically correct.

1. **Je travaille de** _____ **en plus.**

2. **Samedi j'ai travaillé du matin** _____ **soir.**

3. **Je n'** _____ **pouvais plus. J'étais très fatigué(e).**

4. **Dimanche je me** _____ **reposé(e).**

5. **Aujourd'hui je** _____ **porte beaucoup mieux.**

III. Write three sentences in French stating that (a) on Saturday you worked from morning until night, (b) you rested on Sunday, (c) today you are feeling much better.

(a) _____

(b) _____

(c) _____

IV. **Mots-croisés** (Crossword Puzzle)

Write the past participle for each of the following verbs listed below the puzzle. Don't forget to use the vocabulary pages in the back of this book. All the past participles you need to know are right next to the verbs in the vocabulary pages.

Verticalement

1. **devoir**
2. **naître**
3. **lire**
4. **vendre**

5. **prendre**
6. **dire**
7. **falloir**
12. **user**

14. **finir**
16. **mourir**
17. **être**
20. **avoir**

Horizontalement

1. **donner**
5. **pouvoir**
7. **fuir**
8. **rire**
9. **devoir (à l'envers)***

10. **taire**
11. **savoir**
13. **lire**
15. **savoir**

18. **naître**
19. **rire (à l'envers)***
21. **taire**
22. **tuer**

*à l'envers / backwards

Write the heading in French.

_____

_____

Qu'est-ce qui est arrivé?

(What happened?)

I.   Write two sentences of your own in French using the expression given.

141. **Qu'est-ce qui est arrivé?**   What happened?   **Qu'est-ce qui est arrivé?**
What happened?

_____

_____

142. **se blesser**   to injure, hurt, wound oneself   **Je me suis blessé(e) dans un accident. Rien de grave.**
I injured myself in an accident. Nothing serious.

_____

_____

143. **C'est dommage.**   That's too bad.   **C'est dommage. Allez-vous mieux maintenant?**
That's too bad. Are you feeling better now?

_____

_____

144. **tout le monde**   everybody   **Tout le monde me pose la même question!**
Everybody asks me the same question!

_____

_____

145. **cesser de (+ infinitive)**   to cease, stop (+ present participle)   **J'ai cessé de pleurer. Tout va bien. Merci.**
I've stopped crying. Everything is all right. Thank you.

_____

_____

II.   On the line write in French one word that will make the sentence meaningful and grammatically correct.

1. **Qu'est- _____ qui est arrivé?**

2. **Je me _____ blessé(e) dans un accident.**

3. **C'est _____. Allez-vous mieux maintenant?**

4. **Tout _____ monde me pose la même question!**

5. **J' _____ cessé de pleurer. Tout va bien. Merci.**

III. A friend of yours was injured in an accident. Write four French words or expressions that you would use while talking about what happened.

1. _____ 3. _____

2. _____ 4. _____

IV. This is a telephone conversation between Madame Paquet and Madame Banluc.

Madame Paquet, on the left, is asking Madame Banluc how she feels. Madame Banluc injured herself in an accident and broke two fingers on her left hand. Write in French the responses according to the directions given in English.

Madame Paquet: **Bonjour! Annie? Ici Monique Paquet. Comment ça va?**

Madame Banluc: _____
(She returns the greeting and says she injured herself.)

Madame Paquet: **Quoi? Tu t'es blessée dans un accident? Quel accident?**

Madame Banluc: _____
(She says in a car accident.)

Madame Paquet: **Oh! C'est dommage. Tu vas mieux maintenant?**

Madame Banluc: _____
(She says everybody is asking her the same question.)

Madame Paquet: **C'est grave?**

Madame Banluc: _____
(She says no, nothing serious.)

Madame Paquet: **Et comment va tout maintenant?**

Madame Banluc: _____
(She says everything is all right now. Thank you.)

Write the heading in French.

_____

_____

J'ai fait des emplettes.

(I did some shopping.)

I. Write two sentences of your own in French using the expression given.

146. **demander**   to ask (for)   **J'ai demandé de l'argent à mon père.**
I asked my father for some money.

_____

_____

147. **d'abord**   at first   **D'abord il a refusé.**
At first he refused.

_____

148. **avoir la bonté de**   to have the   **Puis, il a eu la bonté de me donner cent**
kindness to   **francs.**
Then he had the kindness to give me
one hundred francs.

_____

149. **faire des emplettes** to do some   **J'ai fait des emplettes.**
shopping   I did some shopping.

_____

_____

150. **tout le temps**   all the time   **Je demande de l'argent à mon père tout**
le temps!
I ask my father for (some) money all the
time!

_____

_____

II. On the line write in French one word that will make the sentence meaningful and grammatically correct.

1. **J'ai** _____ **de l'argent à mon père.**

2. **D'abord il a** _____ .

3. **Puis, il a** _____ **la bonté de me donner cent francs.**

4. **J'ai** _____ **des emplettes.**

5. **Je** _____ **de l'argent à mon père tout le temps!**

III. Answer the following questions in French. You do not have to write a complete sentence with a subject and verb. Just two or three words, maybe even four, are enough. Your answers must show that you understood the questions. What you write must be comprehensible.

1. **D'habitude, à qui demandez-vous de l'argent?** _____
_____

2. **Combien d'argent est-ce que votre père vous a donné?** _____
_____

3. **Qu'est-ce que vous avez fait avec l'argent?** _____
_____

IV. Write a short paragraph in French containing three sentences. State (a) whom you asked for money (b) how much he or she gave you, and (c) what you did with the money.

_____

_____

_____

V. Look at the picture. Then, write in French what is asked for in the directions.

A. Write four French words or expressions to describe the scene.

1. _____ 3. _____

2. _____ 4. _____

B. Write in French four things that the girl bought when she went shopping. A new coat that she's wearing? New boots? A pretty dress in her shopping bag?

1. _____ 3. _____

2. _____ 4. _____

VI. **Lists.** You are planning to shop for a holiday weekend. Write a list of groceries that you need to buy.

1. _____ 3. _____ 5 _____

2. _____ 4. _____ 6. _____

Write the heading in French.

_____

_____

I. Write three sentences in French stating that (a) on Saturday you worked from morning until night, (b) you rested on Sunday, (c) today you are feeling much better.

(a) _____

(b) _____

(c) _____

II. Write a short paragraph in French containing three sentences. State (a) whom you asked for money (b) how much he or she gave you, and (c) what you did with the money.

_____

_____

_____

_____

_____

_____

III. Look at the picture. Then, write in French what is asked for in the directions.

A. Write four French words or expressions to describe the scene.

1. _____ 3. _____

2. _____ 4. _____

B. Write in French four things that the girl bought when she went shopping. A new coat that she's wearing? New boots? A pretty dress in her shopping bag?

1. _____ 3. _____

2. _____ 4. _____

IV. A friend of yours was injured in an accident. Write four French words or expressions that you would use while talking about what happened.

1. _____   3. _____

2. _____   4. _____

V. This is a telephone conversation between Madame Paquet and Madame Banluc.

Madame Paquet, on the left, is asking Madame Banluc how she feels. Madame Banluc injured herself in an accident and broke two fingers on her left hand. Write in French the responses according to the directions given in English.

Madame Paquet: **Bonjour! Annie? Ici Monique Paquet. Comment ça va?**

Madame Banluc: _____
(She returns the greeting and says she injured herself.)

Madame Paquet: **Quoi? Tu t'es blessée dans un accident? Quel accident?**

Madame Banluc: _____
(She says in a car accident.)

Madame Paquet: **Oh! C'est dommage. Tu vas mieux maintenant?**

Madame Banluc: _____
(She says everybody is asking her the same question.)

Madame Paquet: **C'est grave?**

Madame Banluc: _____
(She says no, nothing serious.)

Madame Paquet: **Et comment va tout maintenant?**

Madame Banluc: _____
(She says everything is all right now. Thank you.)

proverbe   **Rira bien qui rira le dernier.**   He who laughs last laughs best.

Write the heading in French.

_____

_____

J'ai reçu un vélo pour mon anniversaire.

(I received a bike for my birthday.)

I.   Write two sentences of your own in French using the expression given.

151. **il y a (+ length of time)** — (length of time) + ago

Je suis né(e) à New York il y a longtemps.
I was born in New York a long time ago.

_____

_____

_____

152. **à la maison** — at home

J'ai célébré mon anniversaire de naissance à la maison le premier avril.
I celebrated my birthday on April first at home.

_____

_____

_____

153. **prier de (+ inf.)** — to beg, ask (+ inf.)

J'ai prié mes parents de me donner un vélo.
I asked my parents to give me a bike.

_____

_____

_____

154. **que . . .** — how . . . (in exclamations)

J'ai reçu un vélo pour mon anniversaire. Qu'il est beau!
I received a bike for my birthday. How beautiful it is!

_____

_____

_____

155. **jusqu'à** — until

Nous avons chanté et dansé jusqu'à minuit.
We sang and danced until midnight.

_____

_____

_____

II. On the line write in French one word that will make the sentence meaningful and grammatically correct.

1. **Je suis né(e) à New York il _____ a longtemps.**

2. **J'ai célébré mon _____ de naissance à la maison.**

3. **J'ai prié mes parents de _____ donner un vélo.**

4. **J'ai _____ un vélo pour mon anniversaire.**

5. **Nous _____ chanté et dansé jusqu'à minuit.**

III. Answer the following questions in French. You do not have to write a complete sentence with a subject and verb. Just two or three words, maybe even four, are enough. Your answers must show that you understood the questions. What you write must be comprehensible.

1. **Quand êtes-vous né(e)?** _____

2. **Où avez-vous célébré votre anniversaire de naissance?** _____

   _____

3. **Qu'est-ce que vous avez reçu pour votre anniveraire?** _____

   _____

IV. Look at the picture. Then, write in French what is asked for in the directions.

A. Write four French words of places where a person rides a bike.

   1. _____   3. _____

   2. _____   4. _____

B. Write four adjectives in French to describe this **vélo.**

   1. _____   3. _____

   2. _____   4. _____

V. Write a note to a friend saying that (a) you celebrated your birthday at home on April first, (b) that you received a bike for your birthday, and (c) that you all sang and danced until midnight. Begin the note with **Cher ami** or **Chère amie** (Dear friend) and end the note with **à bientôt** (see you soon). Then write your name. Don't forget to write the date in French!

_____

_____

_____

_____

_____

_____

_____

_____

_____

_____

Write the complete heading in French.

_____

_____

Une dame est sortie d'une boulangerie.

(A woman came out of a bakery shop.)

I. Write two sentences of your own in French using the expression given.

156. **sortir de**   to come out of, to go out of, to leave   **Une dame est sortie d'une boulangerie.**
A woman came out of a bakery shop.

_____

_____

157. **s'arrêter**   to stop   **Elle s'est arrêtée devant la boutique.**
She stopped in front of the shop.

_____

_____

158. **s'approcher de**   to approach   **Une autre dame s'est approchée d'elle.**
Another woman approached her.

_____

_____

159. **se mettre à (+ inf.)**   to begin to   **Elles se sont mises à parler.**
They began to talk.

_____

_____

160. **sans doute**   undoubtedly, doubtless, without a doubt   **Sans doute elles étaient amies.**
Undoubtedly they were friends.

_____

_____

II. On the line write in French one word that will make the sentence meaningful and grammatically correct.

1. **Une dame** _____ **sortie d'une boulangerie.**

2. **Elle s'** _____ **arrêtée devant la boutique.**

3. **Une autre dame s'** _____ **approchée d'elle.**

4. **Elles se** _____ **mises à parler.**

5. **Sans** _____ **elles étaient amies.**

III. Answer the following questions in French. You do not have to write a complete sentence with a subject and verb. Just two or three words, maybe even four, are enough. Your answers must show that you understood the questions. What you write must be comprehensible.

1. **Qui est sorti de la boulangerie?** _____

_____

2. **Où est-ce que la femme s'est arrêtée?** _____

_____

3. **Qui s'est approché de la femme?** _____

_____

IV. **Lists.** Write French words and expressions according to the directions.

A. Write four French verbs used in this lesson.

1. _____ 3. _____

2. _____ 4. _____

B. Write two French words naming things a person can buy in a **boulangerie.**

1. _____ 2. _____

C. Write four French words or expressions that you would use to describe the picture shown here.

1. _____ 3. _____

2. _____ 4. _____

Write the complete heading in French.

_____

_____

La petite fille a mis le nouveau chapeau de sa mère.
(The little girl put on her mother's new hat.)

I. Write two sentences of your own in French using the expression given.

161. **mettre**   to put on   **La petite fille a mis le nouveau chapeau de sa mère.**
The little girl put on her mother's new hat.

_____

_____

162. **tout à coup**   suddenly   **Tout à coup, sa mère est entrée dans la chambre.**
Suddenly her mother came into the room.

_____

_____

163. **se fâcher**   to get angry   **Sa mère s'est fâchée.**
Her mother got angry.

_____

_____

164. **tout de suite**   immediately   **La petite fille a commencé à pleurer tout de suite.**
Immediately the little girl began to cry.

_____

_____

165. **à l'instant**   instantly, at once   **A l'instant sa mère a mis le chapeau dans la boîte.**
At once her mother put the hat in the box.

_____

_____

II. Answer the following questions in French. You do not have to write a complete sentence with a subject and verb. Just two or three words, maybe even four, are enough. Your answers must show that you understood the questions. What you write must be comprehensible.

1. **Qui a mis le nouveau chapeau de la mère?** _____

2. **Qui est entré dans la chambre tout à coup?** _____

3. **Qui s'est fâché?** _____

4. **Qu'est-ce que la petite fille a fait tout de suite?** _____

5. **Qu'est-ce que la mère a fait à l'instant?** _____

III. Look at the picture shown below. Then write six French words and expressions that you would use to describe it.

A l'heure des petites filles en fleurs

Des petites robes d'été pratiques
comme des tee-shirts, faciles à porter, et très romantiques.

ROBE coton,
haut style "Tee-shirt",
jupe et manches
toile écrue imprimée
"fleurs".
Coloris écru/rose
ou écru/bleu.
Du 18 mois au 8 ans.
Le 4 ans.

AUX TROIS
QUARTIERS

boulevard de la Madeleine
ouvert tous les jours de 9 h 45 à 18 h 30
4 parkings gratuits :
Madeleine, Concorde,
Garages de Paris, Malesherbes

1. _____   4. _____

2. _____   5. _____

3. _____   6. _____

Write the complete heading in French.

_____

_____

I.   Look at the picture. Then, write in French what is asked for in the directions.

A. Write in French four places where a person rides a bike.

1. _____   3. _____

2. _____   4. _____

B. Write four adjectives in French to describe this **vélo.**

1. _____   3. _____

2. _____   4. _____

II.   Write a note to a friend saying that (a) you celebrated your birthday at home on April first, (b) that you received a bike for your birthday, and (c) that you all sang and danced until midnight. Begin the note with **Cher ami** or **Chère amie** (Dear friend) and end the note with **à bientôt** (see you soon). Then write your name. Don't forget to write the date in French!

_____

_____

_____

_____

_____

_____

_____

_____

_____

_____

III.   Answer the following questions in French. You do not have to write a complete sentence with a subject and verb. Just two or three words, maybe even four, are enough. Your answers must show that you understood the questions. What you write must be comprehensible.

1. **Qui est sorti de la boulangerie?** _____

_____

2. **Où est-ce que la femme s'est arrêtée?** _____

_____

3. **Qui s'est approché de la femme?** _____

_____

Review Test 11   **89**

IV. Answer the following questions in French. You do not have to write a complete sentence with a subject and verb. Just two or three words, maybe even four, are enough. Your answers must show that you understood the questions. What you write must be comprehensible.

1. **Qui a mis le nouveau chapeau de la mère?** _____

_____

2. **Qui est entré dans la chambre tout à coup?** _____

_____

3. **Qui s'est fâché?** _____

4. **Qu'est-ce que la petite fille a fait tout de suite?** _____

_____

5. **Qu'est-ce que la mère a fait à l'instant?** _____

_____

V. **Lists.** Write French words and expressions according to the directions.

A. Write in French two things a person can buy in a **boulangerie.**

1. _____ 2. _____

B. Write four French words or expressions that you would use to describe the picture shown here.

1. _____ 3. _____

2. _____ 4. _____

proverbe **Tout est bien qui finit bien.** All's well that ends well.

Write the complete heading in French.

_____

_____

Je suis allé(e) à l'Opéra.
(I went to the Opera.)

I. Write two sentences of your own in French using the expression given.

166. **faire la connais-**   to meet (someone   **Cher ami: J'ai fait la connaissance de**
     sance   for the first time)   **beaucoup de personnes ici à Paris.**
                                                          Dear friend: I've met many people here in
                                                          Paris.

                                                         _____

                                                         _____

167. **encore une fois**   once more   **Je suis allé(e) à l'Opéra encore une fois.**
                                                         I went to the Opera once more.

                                                         _____

                                                         _____

168. **à propos**   by the way   **A propos, aimes-tu l'opéra?**
                                                         By the way, do you like opera?

                                                         _____

                                                         _____

169. **oublier de (+ inf.)**   to forget to (+ inf.)   **N'oublie pas d'écrire.**
                                                         Don't forget to write.

                                                         _____

                                                         _____

170. **à bientôt**   see you soon   **A bientôt.**
                                                         See you soon.

                                                         _____

                                                         _____

II. On the line write in French one word that will make the sentence meaningful and grammatically correct.

1. **Cher ami: J'ai** _____ **la connaissance de beaucoup de personnes ici a Paris.**

2. **Je** _____ **allé(e) à l'Opéra encore une fois.**

3. **A propos, aimes-**_____ **l'opéra?**

4. **N'oublie** _____ **d'écrire.**

5. _____ **bientôt.**

III. Answer the following questions in French. You do not have to write a complete sentence with a subject and a verb. Just two or three words, maybe even four, are enough. Your answers must show that you understood the questions. What you write must be comprehensible.

1. **Où avez-vous fait la connaissance de votre meilleur(e) ami(e)?** _____

_____

2. **Où allez-vous pour entendre de la musique?** _____

_____

3. **Nommez deux instruments de musique.** _____

_____

IV. **Lists.** Look at the picture. Then, write in French what is asked for in the directions.

A. Write the names of two places where the actor is performing. At the opera? At the theater?

1. _____ 2. _____

B. Write four words that you would use to describe this scene.

1. _____ 3. _____

2. _____ 4. _____

V. You are a tourist in Paris. Write a post card to a friend saying that you have met many people in Paris and that you went to the Opera. Also, ask your friend if he or she likes opera. Tell your friend not to forget to write. Begin the note with **Cher ami** or **Chère amie** and end the note with **à bientôt.** Then write your name. Don't forget to write the date in French!

Write the complete heading in French.

_____

_____

Je pense à ce poème.

(I'm thinking about this poem.)

I. Write two sentences of your own in French using the expression given.

171. **penser à** to think of (about) **A quoi pensez-vous? Je pense à ce poème.**
What are you thinking about? I'm thinking about this poem.

_____

_____

172. **avoir le temps de** to have time to **Je n'ai pas le temps de l'étudier maintenant.**
I don't have time to study it now.

_____

_____

173. **tout à l'heure** in a little while, a little while ago **Je vais l'étudier tout à l'heure.**
I'm going to study it in a little while.

_____

_____

174. **penser de** to think of (about) (asking opinion) **Que pensez-vous de ce poème? Je le trouve beau.**
What do you think of this poem? I find it beautiful.

_____

_____

175. **apprendre par coeur** to memorize, to learn by heart **Apprenez-le par coeur!**
Learn it by heart!

_____

_____

II. On the line write in French one word that will make the sentence meaningful and grammatically correct.

1. **A quoi pensez-vous? Je pense** _____ **ce poème.**

2. **Je n'ai** _____ **le temps de l'étudier maintenant.**

3. **Je vais l'étudier** _____ **à l'heure.**

4. **Que pensez-vous** _____ **ce poème? Je le trouve beau!**

5. **Apprenez-le** _____ **coeur!**

Je pense à ce poème **93**

III. Answer the following questions in French. You do not have to write a complete sentence with a subject and verb. Just two or three words, maybe even four, are enough. Your answers must show that you understood the questions. What you write must be comprehensible. As for the three proverbs you are asked to write in French, they must be complete.

1. **A quoi pensez-vous à ce moment?** _____

_____

2. **Quel poème avez-vous appris par coeur?** _____

_____

3. **Ecrivez trois proverbes en français.**

    (a) _____

    (b) _____

    (c) _____

IV. Look at the picture of the man thinking. Then, write three or four words in French to complete the statement.

1. **Le monsieur pense à** _____.

V. Look again at the picture of the man thinking. Then, write four adjectives in French to describe him.

1. _____ 3. _____

2. _____ 4. _____

VI. How many French words can you find hidden in the French word **PENSEUR** (thinker)? Find at least six and write them on the lines.

$$\boxed{\textbf{P E N S E U R}}$$

1. _____ 4. _____

2. _____ 5. _____

3. _____ 6. _____

Write the complete heading in French.

_____

_____

Je vais tout à fait bien.

(I am quite well.)

I. Write two sentences of your own in French using the expression given.

176. **Comment ça va?**   How are things?   **Cher ami: Comment ça va? Chère amie: Comment ça va?**
Dear friend: How are things?

_____

_____

177. **tout à fait**   quite, completely   **Je vais tout à fait bien.**
I am quite well.

_____

_____

178. **hier soir**   last night, yesterday evening   **Je suis arrivé(e) à Paris hier soir. Je m'amuse beaucoup.**
I arrived in Paris last night. I'm having lots of fun.

_____

_____

179. **quelque chose à (+ inf.)**   something to (+ inf.)   **J'ai quelque chose à te dire quand je te verrai.**
I have something to tell you when I see you.

_____

_____

180. **Au revoir**   good-bye   **Au revoir. A bientôt.**
Good-bye. See you soon.

_____

_____

II. On the line write in French one word that will make the sentence meaningful and grammatically correct.

1. **Comment** _____ **va?**

2. **Je vais** _____ **à fait bien.**

3. **Je** _____ **arrivé(e) à Paris hier soir.**

4. **J'ai quelque chose** _____ **te dire quand je te verrai.**

5. **Au** _____ **. A bientôt.**

III. You have just arrived in Paris where you are going to spend one year studying at the **Université de Paris.** You are looking for an apartment in the classified ads of a French newspaper. Read it, then answer the questions in three or four words in French.

```
┌─────────────────────────────┐
│      BEL APPARTEMENT        │
│      belle vue de Paris     │
│      2 chambres, 2 bains    │
│  cuisine moderne, grand balcon │
│        à Montparnasse       │
│      tél. 45-04-55-14       │
└─────────────────────────────┘
```

1. **Où se trouve l'appartement?** _____

2. **Combien de chambres y a-t-il?** _____

3. **Combien de bains?** _____

4. **Est-ce que l'appartment est grand ou petit?** _____

_____

5. **Quel est le numéro de téléphone?** _____

_____

IV. You are leaving for Paris by plane. Here is a copy of your boarding pass. Examine it, then answer the questions.

```
┌──────────────────────────────────────────────────────────────┐
│  CARTE D'ACCES A BORD      NOM DU PASSAGER _____      │
│  (Boarding Pass)           (Passenger's Name)                  │
│                                                                │
│  BAGAGES    COMBIEN DE PIECES    ┌───┐   EMBARQUEMENT (Boarding)│
│  (Baggage)  (How many items)     │ 3 │                         │
│                                  └───┘                         │
│  CORRESPONDANCE      ┌──────────┐      ┌──────────┐            │
│  (Connecting Flight) │  DIRECT  │      │ 13 H. 25 │            │
│                      └──────────┘      └──────────┘            │
│              NEW YORK à PARIS      HEURE (Time)                 │
│                                                                │
│  DATE (Date) 21 JUL      SIEGE (Seat)                          │
│                                                                │
│  VOL (Flight)  ┌────────┐  ┌────────┐  ┌────────┐             │
│                │  077   │  │  23-H  │  │   25   │             │
│                └────────┘  └────────┘  └────────┘             │
│                                        PORTE (Gate)            │
└──────────────────────────────────────────────────────────────┘
```

A. Write the French words for the English words.

1. **Boarding Pass** _____   4. **Connecting Flight** _____

2. **Flight** _____   5. **Gate** _____

3. **Boarding** _____   6. **Seat** _____

B. Write four French words or expressions that you would use while talking to the desk clerk at the airport.

1. _____   3. _____

2. _____   4. _____

C. 1. **At what time do you board the plane?** _____

_____

2. **What is your seat number?** _____

Write the complete heading in French.

_____

_____

I.   You are a tourist in Paris. Write a post card to a friend saying that you have met many people in Paris and that you went to the Opera. Also, ask your friend if he or she likes opera. Tell your friend not to forget to write. Begin the note with **Cher ami** or **Chère amie** and end the note with **à bientôt.** Then write your name. Don't forget to write the date in French!

II. Answer the following questions in French. You do not have to write a complete sentence with a subject and verb. Just two or three words, maybe even four, are enough. Your answers must show that you understood the questions. What you write must be comprehensible. As for the three proverbs you are asked to write in French, they must be complete.

1. **A quoi pensez-vous en ce moment?** _____

_____

2. **Quel poème avez-vous appris par coeur?** _____

_____

3. **Ecrivez trois proverbes en français.**

   (a) _____

   (b) _____

   (c) _____

III. On the line write in French one word that will make the sentence meaningful and grammatically correct.

1. **Comment** _____ **va?**

2. **Je vais** _____ **à fait bien.**

3. **Je** _____ **arrivé(e) à Paris hier soir.**

4. **J'ai quelque chose** _____ **te dire quand je te verrai.**

5. **Au** _____ **. A bientôt.**

IV. You are leaving for Paris by plane. Here is a copy of your boarding pass. Examine it, then answer the questions.

```
┌────────────────────────────────────────────────────────────────────────┐
│  CARTE D'ACCES A BORD       NOM DU PASSAGER _____      │
│  (Boarding Pass)            (Passenger's Name)                           │
│                                                                          │
│  BAGAGES      COMBIEN DE PIECES   ┌───┐   EMBARQUEMENT (Boarding)        │
│  (Baggage)    (How many items)    │ 3 │                                  │
│                                   └───┘                                  │
│  CORRESPONDANCE      ┌──────────┐        ┌──────────┐                    │
│  (Connecting Flight) │  DIRECT  │        │ 13 H. 25 │                    │
│                      └──────────┘        └──────────┘                    │
│              NEW YORK à PARIS          HEURE (Time)                       │
│                                                                          │
│  DATE (Date) 21 JUL        SIEGE (Seat)                                  │
│  VOL (Flight)  ┌────────┐  ┌────────┐    ┌────────┐                      │
│                │  077   │  │  23-H  │    │   25   │                      │
│                └────────┘  └────────┘    └────────┘                      │
│                                          PORTE (Gate)                    │
└────────────────────────────────────────────────────────────────────────┘
```

A. Write the French words for the English words.

1. **Boarding Pass** _____   4. **Connecting Flight** _____

2. **Flight** _____   5. **Gate** _____

3. **Boarding** _____   6. **Seat** _____

B. Write four French words or expressions that you would use while talking to the desk clerk at the airport.

1. _____   3. _____

2. _____   4. _____

C. 1. **At what time do you board the plane? A.M.? or P.M.?** _____

_____

2. **What is your seat number?** _____

_____

3. **Do you have to change planes at another airport?** _____

_____

4. **What is the flight number?** _____

_____

5. **From what city are you leaving and to what city are you going?** _____

_____

proverbe **N'éveillez pas le chat qui dort.** Let sleeping dogs lie.

Write the complete heading in French.

J'aime bien aller en vacances.
(I like going on vacation.)

I.   Write two sentences of your own in French using the expression given.

181. **dans huit jours**   in a week   **J'irai à Paris dans huit jours.**
In a week I will go to Paris.

_____

_____

182. **dans quinze jours**   in two weeks   **Je partirai pour Londres dans quinze jours.**
In two weeks I will leave for London.

_____

_____

183. **s'en aller**   to go away   **Cet été je m'en irai à la campagne.**
This summer I will go away to the country.

_____

_____

184. **ça et là**   here and there   **A la campagne je me promènerai ça et là.**
I will take walks here and there in the country.

_____

_____

185. **en vacances**   on vacation   **J'aime bien aller en vacances.**
I like going on vacation.

_____

_____

II.   On the line write in French one word that will make the sentence meaningful and grammatically correct.

1. **J'irai à Paris** _____ **huit jours.**

2. **Je m'en irai à la campagne** _____ **été.**

3. **Je me promènerai** _____ **et** _____.

4. **J'aime bien** _____ **en vacances.**

III. Look at the picture below. The woman is looking for certain things to pack in her suitcase because she's going on vacation. Tell where she plans to go, how long she will stay there, and what she will do. On the lines under the picture write six French words or expressions that you would use while telling the story.

1. _____ 3. _____ 5. _____

2. _____ 4. _____ 6. _____

IV. **Expressing personal feelings.** You are going on vacation this summer with a friend. You prefer to go to a beach but your friend wants to go camping in the mountains. On the lines below, write four words or expressions in French as reasons why you prefer to go to a beach and not camping in the mountains.

1. _____ 3. _____

2. _____ 4. _____

V. **Providing/obtaining information.** You are in a store looking at clothes to buy because you are going on vacation. You are telling the salesperson what you are looking for and you are asking for suggestions. On the lines below, write four words or expressions in French that you would use in this conversation.

1. _____ 3. _____

2. _____ 4. _____

Write the complete heading in French.

_____

_____

J'ai mangé au moins quatre tartes.

(I ate at least four tarts.)

I. Write two sentences of your own in French using the expression given.

186. **au moins**   at least   **Hier soir je suis descendu(e) dans la cuisine pour goûter un peu. J'ai mangé au moins quatre tartes.**
Last night I went down to the kitchen to have a snack. I ate at least four tarts.

_____

_____

187. **avoir mal à**   to have a pain or ache (in)   **Je suis monté(e) chez moi. J'avais mal à l'estomac.**
I went up to my room. I had a stomach ache.

_____

_____

188. **rester**   to remain, stay   **Je suis resté(e) dans ma chambre.**
I stayed in my room.

_____

_____

189. **tâcher de (+ inf.)**   to try to (+ inf.)   **J'ai tâché de finir un conte.**
I tried to finish a story.

_____

_____

190. **finir par (+ inf.)**   to end up by (+ pres. part.)   **J'ai fini par dormir.**
I ended up by sleeping.

_____

_____

II. On the line write in French the words that will make the sentences meaningful and grammatically correct.

1. **Hier soir je** _____ **descendu(e) dans la cuisine.**

   J'ai mangé _____ **moins quatre tartes.**

2. **J'avais** _____ **à l'estomac.**

3. **Je** _____ **resté(e) dans ma chambre.**

4. **J'ai tâché** _____ **finir un conte.**

5. **J'ai fini** _____ **dormir.**

III. Mots-croisés. This activity tests your knowledge of the **passé composé** tense. The missing words are the present tense of **avoir** or **être** or the correct form of the past participle, or a subject pronoun. You can get help to write in the missing French words in this crossword puzzle by reviewing all previous lessons and by consulting the vocabulary and appendix pages in the back of this book.

Horizontalement

1. **Hier, je** _____ **allé au cinéma.**
3. **Martine est** _____ **(aller) aux grands magasins.**
8. **Pierre** _____ **lu un livre.**
9. **Ils ont** _____ **(vouloir) partir.**
11. _____ **avez parlé assez.**
13. **La lettre? Je l'ai** _____ **(lire).**
14. **Pierre s'est** _____ **(taire).**
15. **J'ai** _____ **(mettre) du sucre dans le café.**

17. **J'ai** _____ **(devoir) (à l'envers)* partir.**
18. **Les lettres? Je les ai** _____ **(mettre) sur le bureau.**
21. **Nous avons bien** _____ **(rire).**
22. **Avez-vous** _____ **(savoir) la réponse?**
23. **Paul a-t-** _____ **compris?**
24. **Qu'a-t-elle** _____ **(dire)?**

Verticalement

1. **Je** _____ **tombé en montant dans le bus.**
2. **J'ai** _____ **(savoir) la réponse.**
3. **Hier soir, j'** _____ **beaucoup mangé.**
4. **Ma camarade a** _____ **(lire) un livre intéressant.**
5. **Ce matin j'ai** _____ **(avoir) un petit accident.**
6. **Nous** _____ **pris le train.**
7. **Les enfants ont** _____ **(pouvoir) manger.**

10. **Nous avons** _____ **(vendre) la maison.**
12. **A-t-il** _____ **(savoir) (à l'envers)* répondre à la question?**
15. **Madame Durand est** _____ **(mourir) la semaine dernière.**
16. **Tu as** _____ **(finir) la leçon?**
19. **Jacqueline** _____ **restée à la maison.**
20. **Tu as** _____ **(savoir) cela, n'est-ce pas?**

***à l'envers**/backwards

***à l'envers**/ backwards

Write the complete heading in French.

Mon père
(My father)

I. Write two sentences of your own in French using the expression given.

191. **jouir de**   to enjoy   **Mon père jouit d'une excellente santé.**
My father enjoys excellent health.

192. **par jour**   daily, per day   **Il gagne cent dollars par jour.**
He earns one hundred dollars a day.

193. **avoir la parole**   to have the floor, to speak   **Quand mon père a la parole, nous écoutons.**
When my father speaks, we listen.

194. **à la fois**   at the same time   **Mon père est à la fois beau et intelligent.**
My father is handsome and at the same time intelligent.

195. **pas du tout**   not at all   **Il n'est pas du tout méchant. Il est président d'une banque.**
He is not at all mean. He is president of a bank.

II. Answer the following questions in French. You do not have to write a complete sentence with a subject and verb. Just two or three words, maybe even four, are enough. Your answers must show that you understood the questions. What you write must be comprehensible.

1. **Quelle est la profession de votre père?** _____

2. **Combine d'heures par jour votre père travaille-t-il?** _____

3. **Que faites-vous quand votre père a la parole?** _____

III. Look at the picture below. The man is late for work. As you can see, he is leaving the house so quickly that he forgot to finish dressing. Tell where he works, what kind of work he does, why he is late for work, what he is holding in both hands, if he is going to take his car or take a bus. You may use these or any ideas of your own. On the lines write eight French words or expressions that you would use in telling a brief story about him.

1. _____
2. _____
3. _____
4. _____
5. _____
6. _____
7. _____
8. _____

Write the complete heading in French.

_____

_____

Comment dit-on *I love you* en français?
On dit *Je t'aime.*

(How do you say *I love you* in French? You say *Je t'aime.*)

I. Write two sentences of your own in French using the expressions given.

196. **comment dit-on . . .**   how do you say . . .   **Comment dit-on *I love you* en français? On dit *je t'aime.*** How do you say *I love you* in French? You say *je t'aime.*

_____

_____

197. **vouloir dire**   to mean   **Que veut dire *tout de suite*? Cela veut dire *immédiatement.*** What does ***tout de suite*** mean? It means *immediately.*

_____

_____

198. **merci infiniment**   thanks a million   **Merci infiniment, monsieur.** Thanks a million, sir.

_____

_____

199. **de rien**   don't mention it   **De rien.**
200. **Il n'y a pas de quoi.**   You're welcome.   **Il n'y a pas de quoi.** You're welcome.

_____

_____

201. **Je vous en prie.**   You're welcome.   **Je vous en prie. Au revoir.** You're welcome. Good-bye.

_____

_____

II. On the line write in French one word that will make the sentence meaningful and grammatically correct.

1. **Comment** _____ -**on** *I love you* **en français?**

2. **On dit** *Je t'* _____ .

3. **Que veut** _____ *tout de suite?*

4. **De** _____ .

5. **Il n'y a pas de** _____ .

6. **Je vous en** _____ .

7. **Au** _____ .

8. **Que** _____ **dire** *immédiatement?*

III. **A Letter Clock.**
Three conjunctions in French are hidden in this clock; one conjunction from 12 to 6; one from 4 to 6; and another from 6 to 11. Note that the same letter can be common to the one that follows. This clock has no hands because it's a "word clock." Write the missing letters on the lines. You can get help to write in the missing letters of the French words in this word game by reviewing all previous lessons and by consulting the vocabulary and appendix pages in the back of this book.

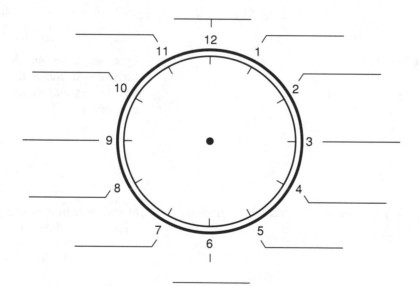

Clues:

• From 12 to 6, give the French for the conjunction "when" that is a synonym of **quand.**

• From 4 to 6, give the French for the conjunction "that."

• From 6 to 11, give the French for the conjunction "at the same time as."

(There was no more room in the clock to write **temps que** to complete that conjunction!)

IV. Unscramble the words to form a coherent sentence.

1. **me / ne / donne / les / Elle / pas** _____

2. **pas / ne / leur / le / Je / donne** _____

3. **leur / Ne / les / pas / donnez** _____

4. **s' / pas / est / lavée / ne / Elle** _____

5. **pas / ai / lui / donné / Je / le / ne** _____

Write the complete heading in French.

_____

_____

I.   Look at the picture below. The woman is looking for certain things to pack in her suitcase because she's going on vacation. Tell where she plans to go, how long she will stay there, and what she will do. On the lines under the picture write six French words or expressions that you would use while telling the story.

1. _____ 2. _____ 3. _____

4. _____ 5. _____ 6. _____

II.   **Expressing personal feelings.** You are going on vacation this summer with a friend. You prefer to go to a beach but your friend wants to go camping in the mountains. On the lines below, write four words or expressions in French as reasons why you prefer to go to a beach and not camping in the mountains.

1. _____ 2. _____

3. _____ 4. _____

III. Answer the following questions in French. You do not have to write a complete sentence with a subject and verb. Just two or three words, maybe even four, are enough. Your answers must show that you understood the questions. What you write must be comprehensible.

1. **Quelle est la profession de votre père?** _____

_____

2. **Combien d'heures par jour votre père travaille-t-il?** _____

_____

3. **Que faites-vous quand votre père a la parole?** _____

_____

IV. Unscramble the words to form a coherent sentence.

1. **me / ne / donne / les / Elle / pas** _____

2. **pas / ne / leur / le / Je / donne** _____

3. **leur / Ne / les / pas / donnez** _____

4. **s' / pas / est / lavée / ne / Elle** _____

5. **pas / ai / lui / donné / Je / le / ne** _____

V. On the line write in French one word which would make the sentence meaningful and grammatically correct.

1. **Comment** _____ **-on** *I love you* **en français?**

2. **On dit** *Je t'* _____ .

3. **Que veut** _____ *tout de suite?*

4. **De** _____ .

5. **Il n'y a pas de** _____ .

6. **Je vous en** _____ .

7. **Au** _____ .

8. **Que** _____ **dire** *immédiatement?*

VI. **Providing/obtaining information.** You are in a store looking at clothes to buy because you are going on vacation. You are telling the salesperson what you are looking for and you are asking for suggestions. On the lines below, write four words or expressions in French that you would use in this conversation.

1. _____   2. _____

3. _____   4. _____

proverbe   **Mieux vaut tard que jamais.**   Better late than never.

Appendix

Optional situations
for conversational
and writing skills as enrichment

◆

Directions: You may talk about these situations in French or write about them, or both.

1. **Ask a friend to go see a movie with you.** Tell what the title of the film is, whether it is in English or French, at what time the movie begins, where you can meet and what you plan to do after the movie.

2. **You have just come home very late.** A member of your family asks you where you were and you have to tell the person that you were in a car accident that wasn't serious.

3. **You are in Paris and you want to spend a few days in the mountains.** You go to a travel agency to get information.

4. **You are going to a birthday party with a friend.** The two of you are in your room figuring out what to wear.

5. **You are taking a walk in Paris with a friend.** You are both deciding where to go first. You are discussing which tourist area is the best.

6. **You are in a drug store in Paris** and you want to buy something for a headache.

7. **You are in a restaurant in Paris for lunch** and you can't decide what to order. The waiter or waitress is getting impatient.

8. **You are in a bookstore in Paris** looking for a specific type of book about France. You find the book, pay for it, and then you ask for the name and address of a good French restaurant that the bookstore clerk can recommend.

9. **You are in a French restaurant for breakfast** and you are trying to decide what to order. Each time the waiter or waitress makes a suggestion, you say you don't like it and you give your reason why.

10. **You go into a pastry shop** and ask the clerk if there are any fresh baked pastries. You ask how much. When you find out how much, you notice that you don't have enough money on you.

11. **You are in an airport in Paris.** You just missed the plane for New York. Ask a clerk for information regarding the next flight to New York City.

12. **You are in Paris looking for the Louvre Museum.** You approach a policeman for directions but he does not understand English and you speak some French.

13. **You are in a bank in Paris** and you want to cash a traveler's check but you don't have any identification with you. Prove to the clerk somehow that you are who you are.

14. **You are having dinner in a cheap restaurant** in a small town in France. You find a fly in the soup. Call the waiter and tell him about it.

15. **You are driving a car with a friend.** You are on a country road in France. All of a sudden the car stops. It's about two o'clock in the morning. You and your French friend talk about what to do.

Sentence structure

Summary of word order of elements in a French declarative sentence in the present tense

SUBJECT	ne	me	le	lui	y	en	VERB	pas
	n'	m'	la	leur				
		te	l'					
		t'	les					
		se						
		s'						
		nous						
		vous						

Models:

Affirmative	Negative
1. **Janine lit le poème.**	1. **Janine ne lit pas le poème.**
Janine le lit.	**Janine ne le lit pas.**
2. **M. Richy me donne le ragoût.**	2. **M. Richy ne me donne pas le ragoût.**

Summary of word order of elements in a French declarative sentence in the passé composé

SUBJECT	ne	me	le	lui	y	en	VERB	pas	past participle
	n'	m'	la	leur			(Auxiliary		
		te	l'				verb		
		t'	les				**avoir** or		
		se					**être** in the		
		s'					present		
		nous					tense)		
		vous							

Models:

Affirmative	Negative
1. **Louis a préparé le dîner.**	1. **Louis n'a pas préparé le dîner.**
Louis l'a préparé.	**Louis ne l'a pas préparé.**
2. **Rita a préparé les salades.**	2. **Rita n'a pas préparé les salades.**
Rita les a préparées.	**Rita ne les a pas préparées.**

Summary of word order of elements in a French affirmative imperative sentence

VERB	le	moi	lui	y	en
	la	m'	leur		
	l'	toi			
	les	t'			
		nous			
		vous			

Models: (Compare these affirmative imperatives with those in the negative below.)

1. **Répondez à la lettre!**
   Répondez-y!

2. **Écrivez la lettre!**
   Écrivez-la!

3. **Donnez-moi le livre!**

4. **Donnez-le à Marie!**

1. Answer the letter!
   Answer it!

2. Write the letter!
   Write it!

3. Give me the book!

4. Give it to Marie!

Summary of word order of elements in a French negative imperative sentence

Ne	me	le	lui	y	en	VERB	pas
N'	m'	la	leur				
	te	l'					
	t'	les					
	nous						
	vous						

Models: (Compare these negative imperatives with those in the affirmative above.)

1. **Ne répondez pas à la lettre!**
   N'y répondez pas!

2. **N'écrivez pas la lettre!**
   Ne l'écrivez pas!

3. **Ne me donnez pas le livre!**

4. **Ne le donnez pas à Marie!**

1. Don't answer the letter!
   Don't answer it!

2. Don't write the letter!
   Don't write it!

3. Don't give me the book!

4. Don't give it to Marie!

Verbs
used in this book

◆

1. **acheter,** to buy, purchase
2. **aimer,** to like, love
3. **aller,** to go
4. **s'en aller,** to go away
5. **s'amuser,** to have a good time
6. **s'appeler,** to call oneself, to be named
7. **apprendre,** to learn
8. **s'approcher,** to approach
9. **s'arrêter,** to stop
10. **arriver,** to arrive, to happen
11. **assembler,** to meet, gather
12. **assister,** to attend
13. **avoir,** to have
14. **se blesser,** to injure oneself
15. **boire,** to drink
16. **se brosser,** to brush oneself
17. **se casser,** to break (leg, etc.)
18. **célébrer,** to celebrate
19. **cesser,** to cease, stop
20. **changer,** to change
21. **chanter,** to sing
22. **se charger,** to take charge
23. **choisir,** to choose, select
24. **commencer,** to begin, start
25. **comprendre,** to understand
26. **continuer,** to continue
27. **copier,** to copy
28. **se coucher,** to go to bed
29. **danser,** to dance
30. **demander,** to request, ask for
31. **demeurer,** to live, reside
32. **descendre,** to go down
33. **désirer,** to desire, wish
34. **devenir,** to become
35. **dîner,** to dine, to have dinner
36. **dire,** to say, tell
37. **donner,** to give
38. **dormir,** to sleep
39. **éclater,** to burst
40. **écouter,** to listen (to)
41. **écrire,** to write
42. **employer,** to use
43. **entendre,** to hear
44. **entrer,** to enter
45. **être,** to be
46. **étudier,** to study
47. **éveiller,** to wake up, awake
48. **se fâcher,** to get angry
49. **faire,** to do, make
50. **fermer,** to close
51. **finir,** to finish
52. **forger,** to forge
53. **gagner,** to earn, win
54. **goûter,** to snack, taste
55. **s'habiller,** to get dressed
56. **habiter,** to live, reside
57. **jouer,** to play
58. **se laver,** to get washed
59. **se lever,** to get up
60. **lire,** to read
61. **manger,** to eat
62. **mentionner,** to mention
63. **mettre,** to put, place, put on
64. **monter,** to go up, mount
65. **naître,** to be born
66. **neiger,** to snow
67. **nommer,** to name
68. **oublier,** to forget
69. **ouvrir,** to open
70. **parler,** to talk, speak
71. **partir,** to leave
72. **passer,** to pass (by), go (by)
73. **payer,** to pay
74. **penser,** to think
75. **plaire,** to please
76. **pleurer,** to cry, weep
77. **pleuvoir,** to rain
78. **se porter,** to feel (health)
79. **poser,** to pose, put
80. **pouvoir,** to be able, can
81. **préférer,** to prefer
82. **prendre,** to take
83. **prier,** to ask, request, beg
84. **se promener,** to take a walk
85. **quitter,** to leave
86. **se rappeler,** to remember, recall
87. **recevoir,** to receive
88. **refuser,** to refuse
89. **regarder,** to look at
90. **rendre,** to render, give back, return
91. **répondre,** to reply, answer
92. **se reposer,** to rest

93. **ressembler,** to resemble
94. **rester,** to stay, remain
95. **revoir,** to see again
96. **rire,** to laugh
97. **risquer,** to risk
98. **savoir,** to know
99. **se servir,** to use, make use of
100. **sortir,** to go out, leave
101. **se souvenir,** to remember
102. **tâcher,** to try
103. **tenir,** to hold, have
104. **terminer,** to finish, terminate
105. **travailler,** to work
106. **traverser,** to cross
107. **se tromper,** to be mistaken
108. **trouver,** to find
109. **se trouver,** to be located
110. **vendre,** to sell
111. **venir,** to come
112. **visiter,** to visit
113. **vivre,** to live
114. **voir,** to see
115. **vouloir,** to want, wish

Twenty-three French verbs
fully conjugated in all the tenses
that you need to use in this book

◆

Subject Pronouns

The subject pronouns for all verb forms on the following pages have been omitted in order to emphasize the verb forms.

The subject pronouns that have been omitted are, as you know, as follows:

singular
1. **je** or **j'**
2. **tu**
3. **il, elle, on**

plural
1. **nous**
2. **vous**
3. **ils, elles**

You realize, of course, that when you use a verb form in the Imperative (Command) you do not use the subject pronoun with it, as is also done in English. Example: **Parlez!** *Speak!* If you use a reflexive verb in the Imperative, drop the subject pronoun but keep the reflexive pronoun. Example: **Lavez-vous!** *Wash yourself!*

The verbs on the following pages are arranged alphabetically with the infinitive at the top of each page. Note that three regular verbs are included of the **-er, -ir,** and **-re** types. They are **donner, finir,** and **vendre.**

aller

to go

Part. pr. **allant**   Part. passé **allé(e)(s)**

The Seven Simple Tenses		The Seven Compound Tenses	
Singular	Plural	Singular	Plural

1   présent de l'indicatif

		8 passé composé	
vais	allons	suis allé(e)	sommes allé(e)s
vas	allez	es allé(e)	êtes allé(e)(s)
va	vont	est allé(e)	sont allé(e)s

2   imparfait de l'indicatif

		9 plus-que-parfait de l'indicatif	
allais	allions	étais allé(e)	étions allé(e)s
allais	alliez	étais allé(e)	étiez allé(e)(s)
allait	allaient	était allé(e)	étaient allé(e)s

3   passé simple

		10 passé antérieur	
allai	allâmes	fus allé(e)	fûmes allé(e)s
allas	allâtes	fus allé(e)	fûtes allé(e)(s)
alla	allèrent	fut allé(e)	furent allé(e)s

4   futur

		11 futur antérieur	
irai	irons	serai allé(e)	serons allé(e)s
iras	irez	seras allé(e)	serez allé(e)(s)
ira	iront	sera allé(e)	seront allé(e)s

5   conditionnel

		12 conditionnel passé	
irais	irions	serais allé(e)	serions allé(e)s
irais	iriez	serais allé(e)	seriez allé(e)(s)
irait	iraient	serait allé(e)	seraient allé(e)s

6   présent du subjonctif

		13 passé du subjonctif	
aille	allions	sois allé(e)	soyons allé(e)s
ailles	alliez	sois allé(e)	soyez allé(e)(s)
aille	aillent	soit allé(e)	soient allé(e)s

7   imparfait du subjonctif

		14 plus-que-parfait du subjonctif	
allasse	allassions	fusse allé(e)	fussions allé(e)s
allasses	allassiez	fusses allé(e)	fussiez allé(e)(s)
allât	allassent	fût allé(e)	fussent allé(e)s

Impératif
va
allons
allez

Common idiomatic expressions using this verb

Comment allez-vous? Je vais bien, je vais mal, je vais mieux.

aller à la pêche   to go fishing
aller à la rencontre de quelqu'un   to go to meet someone
aller à pied   to walk, to go on foot
aller au fond des choses   to get to the bottom of things
Ça va?   Is everything O.K.? **Oui, ça va!**

s'asseoir

to sit down

Part. pr. **s'asseyant**   Part. passé **assis(e)(es)**

The Seven Simple Tenses		The Seven Compound Tenses	
Singular	Plural	Singular	Plural
1 présent de l'indicatif		**8 passé composé**	
m'assieds	nous asseyons	me suis assis(e)	nous sommes assis(es)
t'assieds	vous asseyez	t'es assis(e)	vous êtes assis(e)(es)
s'assied	s'asseyent	s'est assis(e)	se sont assis(es)
2 imparfait de l'indicatif		**9 plus-que-parfait de l'indicatif**	
m'asseyais	nous asseyions	m'étais assis(e)	nous étions assis(es)
t'asseyais	vous asseyiez	t'étais assis(e)	vous étiez assis(e)(es)
s'asseyait	s'asseyaient	s'était assis(e)	s'étaient assis(es)
3 passé simple		**10 passé antérieur**	
m'assis	nous assîmes	me fus assis(e)	nous fûmes assis(es)
t'assis	vous assîtes	te fus assis(e)	vous fûtes assis(e)(es)
s'assit	s'assirent	se fut assis(e)	se furent assis(es)
4 futur		**11 futur antérieur**	
m'assiérai	nous assiérons	me serai assis(e)	nous serons assis(es)
t'assiéras	vous assiérez	te seras assis(e)	vous serez assis(e)(es)
s'assiéra	s'assiéront	se sera assis(e)	se seront assis(es)
5 conditionnel		**12 conditionnel passé**	
m'assiérais	nous assiérions	me serais assis(e)	nous serions assis(es)
t'assiérais	vous assiériez	te serais assis(e)	vous seriez assis(e)(es)
s'assiérait	s'assiéraient	se serait assis(e)	se seraient assis(es)
6 présent du subjonctif		**13 passé du subjonctif**	
m'asseye	nous asseyions	me sois assis(e)	nous soyons assis(es)
t'asseyes	vous asseyiez	te sois assis(e)	vous soyez assis(e)(es)
s'asseye	s'asseyent	se soit assis(e)	se soient assis(es)
7 imparfait du subjonctif		**14 plus-que-parfait du subjonctif**	
m'assisse	nous assissions	me fusse assis(e)	nous fussions assis(es)
t'assisses	vous assissiez	te fusses assis(e)	vous fussiez assis(e)(es)
s'assît	s'assissent	se fût assis(e)	se fussent assis(es)

Impératif
assieds-toi; ne t'assieds pas
asseyons-nous; ne nous asseyons pas
asseyez-vous; ne vous asseyez pas

Common idiomatic expressions using this verb and words related to it

Quand je voyage dans un train, je m'assieds toujours près d'une fenêtre si c'est possible.
Une fois, pendant un voyage, une belle jeune fille s'est approchée de moi et m'a demandé:
—Puis-je m'asseoir ici? Est-ce que cette place est libre?
—Certainement, j'ai répondu—asseyez-vous, je vous en prie.
Elle s'est assise auprès de moi et nous nous sommes bien amusés à raconter des histoires drôles.

asseoir qqn   to seat someone; **se rasseoir**   to sit down again
rasseoir   to seat again, to reseat

avoir

to have

Part. pr. **ayant**   Part. passé **eu**

The Seven Simple Tenses	
Singular	Plural

1   présent de l'indicatif

ai	avons
as	avez
a	ont

2   imparfait de l'indicatif

avais	avions
avais	aviez
avait	avaient

3   passé simple

eus	eûmes
eus	eûtes
eut	eurent

4   futur

aurai	aurons
auras	aurez
aura	auront

5   conditionnel

aurais	aurions
aurais	auriez
aurait	auraient

6   présent du subjonctif

aie	ayons
aies	ayez
ait	aient

7   imparfait du subjonctif

eusse	eussions
eusses	eussiez
eût	eussent

The Seven Compound Tenses	
Singular	Plural

8   passé composé

ai eu	avons eu
as eu	avez eu
a eu	ont eu

9   plus-que-parfait de l'indicatif

avais eu	avions eu
avais eu	aviez eu
avait eu	avaient eu

10   passé antérieur

eus eu	eûmes eu
eus eu	eûtes eu
eut eu	eurent eu

11   futur antérieur

aurai eu	aurons eu
auras eu	aurez eu
aura eu	auront eu

12   conditionnel passé

aurais eu	aurions eu
aurais eu	auriez eu
aurait eu	auraient eu

13   passé du subjonctif

aie eu	ayons eu
aies eu	ayez eu
ait eu	aient eu

14   plus-que-parfait du subjonctif

eusse eu	eussions eu
eusses eu	eussiez eu
eût eu	eussent eu

Impératif
aie
ayons
ayez

Common idiomatic expressions using this verb

avoir. . . ans   to be . . . years old
avoir à + inf.   to have to, to be obliged to + inf.
avoir besoin de   to need, to have need of
avoir chaud   to be (feel) warm (persons)
avoir froid   to be (feel) cold (persons)

avoir sommeil   to be (feel) sleepy
avoir qqch à faire   to have something to do
avoir de la chance   to be lucky
avoir faim   to be hungry
avoir soif   to be thirsty

comprendre

to understand

Part. pr. **comprenant**   Part. passé **compris**

The Seven Simple Tenses		The Seven Compound Tenses	
Singular	Plural	Singular	Plural

1   présent de l'indicatif

		8 passé composé	
comprends	comprenons	ai compris	avons compris
comprends	comprenez	as compris	avez compris
comprend	comprennent	a compris	ont compris

2   imparfait de l'indicatif

		9 plus-que-parfait de l'indicatif	
comprenais	comprenions	avais compris	avions compris
comprenais	compreniez	avais compris	aviez compris
comprenait	comprenaient	avait compris	avaient compris

3   passé simple

		10 passé antérieur	
compris	comprîmes	eus compris	eûmes compris
compris	comprîtes	eus compris	eûtes compris
comprit	comprirent	eut compris	eurent compris

4   futur

		11 futur antérieur	
comprendrai	comprendrons	aurai compris	aurons compris
comprendras	comprendrez	auras compris	aurez compris
comprendra	comprendront	aura compris	auront compris

5   conditionnel

		12 conditionnel passé	
comprendrais	comprendrions	aurais compris	aurions compris
comprendrais	comprendriez	aurais compris	auriez compris
comprendrait	comprendraient	aurait compris	auraient compris

6   présent du subjonctif

		13 passé du subjonctif	
comprenne	comprenions	aie compris	ayons compris
comprennes	compreniez	aies compris	ayez compris
comprenne	comprennent	ait compris	aient compris

7   imparfait du subjonctif

		14 plus-que-parfait du subjonctif	
comprisse	comprissions	eusse compris	eussions compris
comprisses	comprissiez	eusses compris	eussiez compris
comprît	comprissent	eût compris	eussent compris

Impératif
comprends
comprenons
comprenez

Sentences using this verb and expressions related to it

   Je ne comprends jamais la maîtresse de biologie. Je n'ai pas compris la leçon d'hier, je ne comprends pas la leçon d'aujourd'hui, et je ne comprendrai jamais rien.

faire comprendre à qqn que. . .   to make it clear to someone that. . .
la compréhension   comprehension, understanding
Ça se comprend   Of course; That is understood
y compris   included, including

se coucher

to go to bed, to lie down

Part. pr. **se couchant** Part. passé **couché(e)(s)**

The Seven Simple Tenses		The Seven Compound Tenses	
Singular	Plural	Singular	Plural

1 présent de l'indicatif

me couche	nous couchons	
te couches	vous couchez	
se couche	se couchent	

8 passé composé

me suis couché(e)	nous sommes couché(e)s
t'es couché(e)	vous êtes couché(e)(s)
s'est couché(e)	se sont couché(e)s

2 imparfait de l'indicatif

me couchais	nous couchions
te couchais	vous couchiez
se couchait	se couchaient

9 plus-que-parfait de l'indicatif

m'étais couché(e)	nous étions couché(e)s
t'étais couché(e)	vous étiez couché(e)(s)
s'était couché(e)	s'étaient couché(e)s

3 passé simple

me couchai	nous couchâmes
te couchas	vous couchâtes
se coucha	se couchèrent

10 passé antérieur

me fus couché(e)	nous fûmes couché(e)s
te fus couché(e)	vous fûtes couché(e)(s)
se fut couché(e)	se furent couché(e)s

4 futur

me coucherai	nous coucherons
te coucheras	vous coucherez
se couchera	se coucheront

11 futur antérieur

me serai couché(e)	nous serons couché(e)s
te seras couché(e)	vous serez couché(e)(s)
se sera couché(e)	se seront couché(e)s

5 conditionnel

me coucherais	nous coucherions
te coucherais	vous coucheriez
se coucherait	se coucheraient

12 conditionnel passé

me serais couché(e)	nous serions couché(e)s
te serais couché(e)	vous seriez couché(e)(s)
se serait couché(e)	se seraient couché(e)s

6 présent du subjonctif

me couche	nous couchions
te couches	vous couchiez
se couche	se couchent

13 passé du subjonctif

me sois couché(e)	nous soyons couché(e)s
te sois couché(e)	vous soyez couché(e)(s)
se soit couché(e)	se soient couché(e)s

7 imparfait du subjonctif

me couchasse	nous couchassions
te couchasses	vous couchassiez
se couchât	se couchassent

14 plus-que-parfait du subjonctif

me fusse couché(e)	nous fussions couché(e)s
te fusses couché(e)	vous fussiez couché(e)(s)
se fût couché(e)	se fussent couché(e)s

Impératif
couche-toi; ne te couche pas
couchon-nous; ne nous couchons pas
couchez-vous; ne vous couchez pas

Sentences using this verb and words related to it

—**Couche-toi, Hélène! Il est minuit. Hier soir tu t'es couchée tard.**
—**Donne-moi ma poupée pour nous coucher ensemble.**

le coucher du soleil sunset
une couche a layer
une couchette bunk, cot
Le soleil se couche The sun is setting.

se recoucher to go back to bed
se coucher tôt to go to bed early
Comme on fait son lit on se couche! You've made your bed; now lie in it!

devoir

to have to, must, ought, owe, should

Part. pr. **devant**   Part. passé **dû (due)**

The Seven Simple Tenses		The Seven Compound Tenses	
Singular	Plural	Singular	Plural
1 présent de l'indicatif		**8 passé composé**	
dois	devons	ai dû	avons dû
dois	devez	as dû	avez dû
doit	doivent	a dû	ont dû
2 imparfait de l'indicatif		**9 plus-que-parfait de l'indicatif**	
devais	devions	avais dû	avions dû
devais	deviez	avais dû	aviez dû
devait	devaient	avait dû	avaient dû
3 passé simple		**10 passé antérieur**	
dus	dûmes	eus dû	eûmes dû
dus	dûtes	eus dû	eûtes dû
dut	durent	eut dû	eurent dû
4 futur		**11 futur antérieur**	
devrai	devrons	aurai dû	aurons dû
devras	devrez	auras dû	aurez dû
devra	devront	aura dû	auront dû
5 conditionnel		**12 conditionnel passé**	
devrais	devrions	aurais dû	aurions dû
devrais	devriez	aurais dû	auriez dû
devrait	devraient	aurait dû	auraient dû
6 présent du subjonctif		**13 passé du subjonctif**	
doive	devions	aie dû	ayons dû
doives	deviez	aies dû	ayez dû
doive	doivent	ait dû	aient dû
7 imparfait du subjonctif		**14 plus-que-parfait du subjonctif**	
dusse	dussions	eusse dû	eussions dû
dusses	dussiez	eusses dû	eussiez dû
dût	dussent	eût dû	eussent dû

Impératif
dois
devons
devez

Common idiomatic expressions using this verb

   Hier soir je suis allé au cinéma avec mes amis. Vous auriez dû venir avec nous. Le film était excellent.

Vous auriez dû venir   You should have come.
le devoir   duty, obligation
les devoirs   homework
Cette grosse somme d'argent est due lundi.

dire

to say, to tell

Part pr. **disant**   Part. passé **dit**

The Seven Simple Tenses		The Seven Compound Tenses	
Singular	Plural	Singular	Plural

1   présent de l'indicatif

Singular	Plural
dis	disons
dis	dites
dit	disent

2   imparfait de l'indicatif

disais	disions
disais	disiez
disait	disaient

3   passé simple

dis	dîmes
dis	dîtes
dit	dirent

4   futur

dirai	dirons
diras	direz
dira	diront

5   conditionnel

dirais	dirions
dirais	diriez
dirait	diraient

6   présent du subjonctif

dise	disions
dises	disiez
dise	disent

7   imparfait du subjonctif

disse	dissions
disses	dissiez
dît	dissent

8   passé composé

Singular	Plural
ai dit	avons dit
as dit	avez dit
a dit	ont dit

9   plus-que-parfait de l'indicatif

avais dit	avions dit
avais dit	aviez dit
avait dit	avaient dit

10   passé antérieur

eus dit	eûmes dit
eus dit	eûtes dit
eut dit	eurent dit

11   futur antérieur

aurai dit	aurons dit
auras dit	aurez dit
aura dit	auront dit

12   conditionnel passé

aurais dit	aurions dit
aurais dit	auriez dit
aurait dit	auraient dit

13   passé du subjonctif

aie dit	ayons dit
aies dit	ayez dit
ait dit	aient dit

14   plus-que-parfait du subjonctif

eusse dit	eussions dit
eusses dit	eussiez dit
eût dit	eussent dit

Impératif
dis
disons
dites

Common idiomatic expressions using this verb

—**Qu'est-ce que vous avez dit? Je n'ai pas entendu.**
—**J'ai dit que je ne vous ai pas entendu. Parlez plus fort.**

c'est-à-dire   that is, that is to say
entendre dire que   to hear it said that
vouloir dire   to mean
dire du bien de   to speak well of

donner

to give

Part. pr. **donnant**   Part. passé **donné**

The Seven Simple Tenses	
Singular	Plural

The Seven Compound Tenses	
Singular	Plural

1 présent de l'indicatif

donne	donnons
donnes	donnez
donne	donnent

8 passé composé

ai donné	avons donné
as donné	avez donné
a donné	ont donné

2 imparfait de l'indicatif

donnais	donnions
donnais	donniez
donnait	donnaient

9 plus-que-parfait de l'indicatif

avais donné	avions donné
avais donné	aviez donné
avait donné	avaient donné

3 passé simple

donnai	donnâmes
donnas	donnâtes
donna	donnèrent

10 passé antérieur

eus donné	eûmes donné
eus donné	eûtes donné
eut donné	eurent donné

4 futur

donnerai	donnerons
donneras	donnerez
donnera	donneront

11 futur antérieur

aurai donné	aurons donné
auras donné	aurez donné
aura donné	auront donné

5 conditionnel

donnerais	donnerions
donnerais	donneriez
donnerait	donneraient

12 conditionnel passé

aurais donné	aurions donné
aurais donné	auriez donné
aurait donné	auraient donné

6 présent du subjonctif

donne	donnions
donnes	donniez
donne	donnent

13 passé du subjonctif

aie donné	ayons donné
aies donné	ayez donné
ait donné	aient donné

7 imparfait du subjonctif

donnasse	donnassions
donnasses	donnassiez
donnât	donnassent

14 plus-que-parfait du subjonctif

eusse donné	eussions donné
eusses donné	eussiez donné
eût donné	eussent donné

Impératif
donne
donnons
donnez

Common idiomatic expressions using this verb and words related to it

donner rendez-vous à qqn   to make an appointment (a date) with someone
donner sur   to look upon: **La salle à manger donne sur un joli jardin**   The dining room looks out upon (faces) a pretty garden.
donner congé à   to grant leave to
abandonner   to abandon; **ordonner**   to order; **pardonner**   to pardon

être

to be

Part. pr. **étant**   Part. passé **été**

The Seven Simple Tenses		The Seven Compound Tenses	
Singular	Plural	Singular	Plural
1 présent de l'indicatif		**8 passé composé**	
suis	sommes	ai été	avons été
es	êtes	as été	avez été
est	sont	a été	ont été
2 imparfait de l'indicatif		**9 plus-que-parfait de l'indicatif**	
étais	étions	avais été	avions été
étais	étiez	avais été	aviez été
était	étaient	avait été	avaient été
3 passé simple		**10 passé antérieur**	
fus	fûmes	eus été	eûmes été
fus	fûtes	eus été	eûtes été
fut	furent	eut été	eurent été
4 futur		**11 futur antérieur**	
serai	serons	aurai été	aurons été
seras	serez	auras été	aurez été
sera	seront	aura été	auront été
5 conditionnel		**12 conditionnel passé**	
serais	serions	aurais été	aurions été
serais	seriez	aurais été	auriez été
serait	seraient	aurait été	auraient été
6 présent du subjonctif		**13 passé du subjonctif**	
sois	soyons	aie été	ayons été
sois	soyez	aies été	ayez été
soit	soient	ait été	aient été
7 imparfait du subjonctif		**14 plus-que-parfait du subjonctif**	
fusse	fussions	eusse été	eussions été
fusses	fussiez	eusses été	eussiez été
fût	fussent	eût été	eussent été

Impératif
sois
soyons
soyez

Common idiomatic expressions using this verb

être en train de + inf.   to be in the act of + pres. part., to be in the process of, to be busy + pres. part.;
  Mon père est en train d'écrire une lettre à mes grands-parents.

être à l'heure   to be on time
être à temps   to be in time
être pressé(e)   to be in a hurry

Je suis à vous   I am at your service.
Je suis d'avis que...   I am of the opinion that...

étudier

to study

Part. pr. **étudiant**   Part. passé **étudié**

The Seven Simple Tenses		The Seven Compound Tenses	
Singular	Plural	Singular	Plural
1 présent de l'indicatif		**8 passé composé**	
étudie	étudions	ai étudié	avons étudié
étudies	étudiez	as étudié	avez étudié
étudie	étudient	a étudié	ont étudié
2 imparfait de l'indicatif		**9 plus-que-parfait de l'indicatif**	
étudiais	étudiions	avais étudié	avions étudié
étudiais	étudiiez	avais étudié	aviez étudié
étudiait	étudiaient	avait étudié	avaient étudié
3 passé simple		**10 passé antérieur**	
étudiai	étudiâmes	eus étudié	eûmes étudié
étudias	étudiâtes	eus étudié	eûtes étudié
étudia	étudièrent	eut étudié	eurent étudié
4 futur		**11 futur antérieur**	
étudierai	étudierons	aurai étudié	aurons étudié
étudieras	étudierez	auras étudié	aurez étudié
étudiera	étudieront	aura étudié	auront étudié
5 conditionnel		**12 conditionnel passé**	
étudierais	étudierions	aurais étudié	aurions étudié
étudierais	étudieriez	aurais étudié	auriez étudié
étudierait	étudieraient	aurait étudié	auraient étudié
6 présent du subjonctif		**13 passé du subjonctif**	
étudie	étudiions	aie étudié	ayons étudié
étudies	étudiiez	aies étudié	ayez étudié
étudie	étudient	ait étudié	aient étudié
7 imparfait du subjonctif		**14 plus-que-parfait du subjonctif**	
étudiasse	étudiassions	eusse étudié	eussions étudié
étudiasses	étudiassiez	eusses étudié	eussiez étudié
étudiât	étudiassent	eût étudié	eussent étudié

Impératif
étudie
étudions
étudiez

Sentences using this verb and words related to it

Je connais une jeune fille qui étudie le piano depuis deux ans. Je connais un garçon qui étudie ses leçons à fond. Je connais un astronome qui étudie les étoiles dans le ciel depuis dix ans.

étudier à fond   to study thoroughly
un étudiant, une étudiante   student
l'étude (*f.*)   study; **les études**   studies
faire ses études   to study, to go to school
à l'étude   under consideration, under study

faire

to do, to make

Part. pr. **faisant**   Part. passé **fait**

The Seven Simple Tenses		The Seven Compound Tenses	
Singular	Plural	Singular	Plural

1 présent de l'indicatif

fais	faisons	
fais	faites	
fait	font	

8 passé composé

ai fait	avons fait
as fait	avez fait
a fait	ont fait

2 imparfait de l'indicatif

faisais	faisions
faisais	faisiez
faisait	faisaient

9 plus-que-parfait de l'indicatif

avais fait	avions fait
avais fait	aviez fait
avait fait	avaient fait

3 passé simple

fis	fîmes
fis	fîtes
fit	firent

10 passé antérieur

eus fait	eûmes fait
eus fait	eûtes fait
eut fait	eurent fait

4 futur

ferai	ferons
feras	ferez
fera	feront

11 futur antérieur

aurai fait	aurons fait
auras fait	aurez fait
aura fait	auront fait

5 conditionnel

ferais	ferions
ferais	feriez
ferait	feraient

12 conditionnel passé

aurais fait	aurions fait
aurais fait	auriez fait
aurait fait	auraient fait

6 présent du subjonctif

fasse	fassions
fasses	fassiez
fasse	fassent

13 passé du subjonctif

aie fait	ayons fait
aies fait	ayez fait
ait fait	aient fait

7 imparfait du subjonctif

fisse	fissions
fisses	fissiez
fît	fissent

14 plus-que-parfait du subjonctif

eusse fait	eussions fait
eusses fait	eussiez fait
eût fait	eussent fait

Impératif
fais
faisons
faites

Common idiomatic expressions using this verb

faire beau   to be beautiful weather
faire chaud   to be warm weather
faire froid   to be cold weather
faire de l'autostop   to hitchhike
faire attention à qqn ou à qqch   to pay
   attention to someone or to something

finir

to finish, to end, to terminate, to complete

Part. pr. **finissant**   Part. passé **fini**

The Seven Simple Tenses		The Seven Compound Tenses	
Singular	Plural	Singular	Plural
1 présent de l'indicatif		**8 passé composé**	
finis	finissons	ai fini	avons fini
finis	finissez	as fini	avez fini
finit	finissent	a fini	ont fini
2 imparfait de l'indicatif		**9 plus-que-parfait de l'indicatif**	
finissais	finissions	avais fini	avions fini
finissais	finissiez	avais fini	aviez fini
finissait	finissaient	avait fini	avaient fini
3 passé simple		**10 passé antérieur**	
finis	finîmes	eus fini	eûmes fini
finis	finîtes	eus fini	eûtes fini
finit	finirent	eut fini	eurent fini
4 futur		**11 futur antérieur**	
finirai	finirons	aurai fini	aurons fini
finiras	finirez	auras fini	aurez fini
finira	finiront	aura fini	auront fini
5 conditionnel		**12 conditionnel passé**	
finirais	finirions	aurais fini	aurions fini
finirais	finiriez	aurais fini	auriez fini
finirait	finiraient	aurait fini	auraient fini
6 présent du subjonctif		**13 passé du subjonctif**	
finisse	finissions	aie fini	ayons fini
finisses	finissiez	aies fini	ayez fini
finisse	finissent	ait fini	aient fini
7 imparfait du subjonctif		**14 plus-que-parfait du subjonctif**	
finisse	finissions	eusse fini	eussions fini
finisses	finissiez	eusses fini	eussiez fini
finît	finissent	eût fini	eussent fini

Impératif
finis
finissons
finissez

Sentences using this verb and words and expressions related to it

finir de + inf.   to finish + pr. part.
J'ai fini de travailler pour aujourd'hui   I have finished working for today.

finir par + inf.   the end up by + pr. part.
Louis a fini par épouser une femme plus âgée que lui   Louis ended up by marrying a woman older than he.

la fin   the end; **la fin de semaine**   weekend; **C'est fini!**   It's all over!
afin de   in order to; **enfin**   finally; **finalement**   finally
mettre fin à   to put an end to; **final, finale**   final; **définir**   to define

se laver

to wash oneself

Part. pr. **se lavant**   Part. passé **lavé(e)(s)**

The Seven Simple Tenses		The Seven Compound Tenses	
Singular	Plural	Singular	Plural
1 présent de l'indicatif		**8 passé composé**	
me lave	nous lavons	me suis lavé(e)	nous sommes lavé(e)s
te laves	vous lavez	t'es lavé(e)	vous êtes lavé(e)(s)
se lave	se lavent	s'est lavé(e)	se sont lavé(e)s
2 imparfait de l'indicatif		**9 plus-que-parfait de l'indicatif**	
me lavais	nous lavions	m'étais lavé(e)	nous étions lavé(e)s
te lavais	vous laviez	t'étais lavé(e)	vous étiez lavé(e)(s)
se lavait	se lavaient	s'était lavé(e)	s'étaient lavé(e)s
3 passé simple		**10 passé antérieur**	
me lavai	nous lavâmes	me fus lavé(e)	nous fûmes lavé(e)s
te lavas	vous lavâtes	te fus lavé(e)	vous fûtes lavé(e)(s)
se lava	se lavèrent	se fut lavé(e)	se furent lavé(e)s
4 futur		**11 futur antérieur**	
me laverai	nous laverons	me serai lavé(e)	nous serons lavé(e)s
te laveras	vous laverez	te seras lavé(e)	vous serez lavé(e)(s)
se lavera	se laveront	se sera lavé(e)	se seront lavé(e)s
5 conditionnel		**12 conditionnel passé**	
me laverais	nous laverions	me serais lavé(e)	nous serions lavé(e)s
te laverais	vous laveriez	te serais lavé(e)	vous seriez lavé(e)(s)
se laverait	se laveraient	se serait lavé(e)	se seraient lavé(e)s
6 présent du subjonctif		**13 passé du subjonctif**	
me lave	nous lavions	me sois lavé(e)	nous soyons lavé(e)s
te laves	vous laviez	te sois lavé(e)	vous soyez lavé(e)(s)
se lave	se lavent	se soit lavé(e)	se soient lavé(e)s
7 imparfait du subjonctif		**14 plus-que-parfait du subjonctif**	
me lavasse	nous lavassions	me fusse lavé(e)	nous fussions lavé(e)s
te lavasses	vous lavassiez	te fusses lavé(e)	vous fussiez lavé(e)(s)
se lavât	se lavassent	se fût lavé(e)	se fussent lavé(e)s

Impératif
lave-toi; ne te lave pas
lavons-nous; ne nous lavons pas
lavez-vous; ne vous lavez pas

Sentences using this verb and words related to it

Tous les matins je me lave. Je me lave le visage, je me lave les mains, le cou et les oreilles. Hier soir je me suis lavé les pieds.
Ma mère m'a demandé:—Henriette, est-ce que tu t'es bien lavée?
Je lui ai répondu:—Oui, maman, je me suis lavée! Je me suis bien lavé les mains!

se lever

to get up

Part. pr. **se levant**   Part. passé **levé(e)(s)**

The Seven Simple Tenses		The Seven Compound Tenses	
Singular	Plural	Singular	Plural
1 présent de l'indicatif		**8 passé composé**	
me lève	nous levons	me suis levé(e)	nous sommes levé(e)s
te lèves	vous levez	t'es levé(e)	vous êtes levé(e)(s)
se lève	se lèvent	s'est levé(e)	se sont levé(e)s
2 imparfait de l'indicatif		**9 plus-que-parfait de l'indicatif**	
me levais	nous levions	m'étais levé(e)	nous étions levé(e)s
te levais	vous leviez	t'étais levé(e)	vous étiez levé(e)(s)
se levait	se levaient	s'était levé(e)	s'étaient levé(e)s
3 passé simple		**10 passé antérieur**	
me levai	nous levâmes	me fus levé(e)	nous fûmes levé(e)s
te levas	vous levâtes	te fus levé(e)	vous fûtes levé(e)(s)
se leva	se levèrent	se fut levé(e)	se furent levé(e)s
4 futur		**11 futur antérieur**	
me lèverai	nous lèverons	me serai levé(e)	nous serons levé(e)s
te lèveras	vous lèverez	te seras levé(e)	vous serez levé(e)(s)
se lèvera	se lèveront	se sera levé(e)	se seront levé(e)s
5 conditionnel		**12 conditionnel passé**	
me lèverais	nous lèverions	me serais levé(e)	nous serions levé(e)s
te lèverais	vous lèveriez	te serais levé(e)	vous seriez levé(e)(s)
se lèverait	se lèveraient	se serait levé(e)	se seraient levé(e)s
6 présent du subjonctif		**13 passé du subjonctif**	
me lève	nous levions	me sois levé(e)	nous soyons levé(e)s
te lèves	vous leviez	te sois levé(e)	vous soyez levé(e)(s)
se lève	se lèvent	se soit levé(e)	se soient levé(e)s
7 imparfait du subjonctif		**14 plus-que-parfait du subjonctif**	
me levasse	nous levassions	me fusse levé(e)	nous fussions levé(e)s
te levasses	vous levassiez	te fusses levé(e)	vous fussiez levé(e)(s)
se levât	se levassent	se fût levé(e)	se fussent levé(e)s

Impératif
lève-toi; ne te lève pas
levons-nous; ne nous levons pas
levez-vous; ne vous levez pas

Sentences using this verb and words related to it

  Caroline est entrée dans le salon. Elle s'est assise, puis elle s'est levée. Après s'être levée, elle a quitté la maison.

lire

to read

Part. pr. **lisant**   Part. passé **lu**

The Seven Simple Tenses		The Seven Compound Tenses	
Singular	Plural	Singular	Plural
1 présent de l'indicatif		**8 passé composé**	
lis	lisons	ai lu	avons lu
lis	lisez	as lu	avez lu
lit	lisent	a lu	ont lu
2 imparfait de l'indicatif		**9 plus-que-parfait de l'indicatif**	
lisais	lisions	avais lu	avions lu
lisais	lisiez	avais lu	aviez lu
lisait	lisaient	avait lu	avaient lu
3 passé simple		**10 passé antérieur**	
lus	lûmes	eus lu	eûmes lu
lus	lûtes	eus lu	eûtes lu
lut	lurent	eut lu	eurent lu
4 futur		**11 futur antérieur**	
lirai	lirons	aurai lu	aurons lu
liras	lirez	auras lu	aurez lu
lira	liront	aura lu	auront lu
5 conditionnel		**12 conditionnel passé**	
lirais	lirions	aurais lu	aurions lu
lirais	liriez	aurais lu	auriez lu
lirait	liraient	aurait lu	auraient lu
6 présent du subjonctif		**13 passé du subjonctif**	
lise	lisions	aie lu	ayons lu
lises	lisiez	aies lu	ayez lu
lise	lisent	ait lu	aient lu
7 imparfait du subjonctif		**14 plus-que-parfait du subjonctif**	
lusse	lussions	eusse lu	eussions lu
lusses	lussiez	eusses lu	eussiez lu
lût	lussent	eût lu	eussent lu

Impératif
lis
lisons
lisez

Words and expressions related to this verb

C'est un livre à lire   It's a book worth reading.
lisible   legible, readable
lisiblement   legibly
lecteur, lectrice   reader (a person who reads)
un lecteur d'épreuves, une lectrice d'épreuves
   proof reader
la lecture   reading

lectures pour la jeunesse   juvenile reading
Dans l'espoir de vous lire . . .
   I hope to receive a letter from you soon.
lire à haute voix   to read aloud
lire à voix basse   to read in a low voice
lire tout bas   to read to oneself
relire   to reread

mettre

to put, to place

Part. pr. **mettant**   Part. passé **mis**

The Seven Simple Tenses	
Singular	Plural

1 présent de l'indicatif

mets	mettons
mets	mettez
met	mettent

2 imparfait de l'indicatif

mettais	mettions
mettais	mettiez
mettait	mettaient

3 passé simple

mis	mîmes
mis	mîtes
mit	mirent

4 futur

mettrai	mettrons
mettras	mettrez
mettra	mettront

5 conditionnel

mettrais	mettrions
mettrais	mettriez
mettrait	mettraient

6 présent du subjonctif

mette	mettions
mettes	mettiez
mette	mettent

7 imparfait du subjonctif

misse	missions
misses	missiez
mît	missent

The Seven Compound Tenses	
Singular	Plural

8 passé composé

ai mis	avons mis
as mis	avez mis
a mis	ont mis

9 plus-que-parfait de l'indicatif

avais mis	avions mis
avais mis	aviez mis
avait mis	avaient mis

10 passé antérieur

eus mis	eûmes mis
eus mis	eûtes mis
eut mis	eurent mis

11 futur antérieur

aurai mis	aurons mis
auras mis	aurez mis
aura mis	auront mis

12 conditionnel passé

aurais mis	aurions mis
aurais mis	auriez mis
aurait mis	auraient mis

13 passé du subjonctif

aie mis	ayons mis
aies mis	ayez mis
ait mis	aient mis

14 plus-que-parfait du subjonctif

eusse mis	eussions mis
eusses mis	eussiez mis
eût mis	eussent mis

Impératif
mets
mettons
mettez

Words and expressions related to this verb

mettre la table   to set the table
mettre de côté   to lay aside, to save
mettre en cause   to question
mettre qqn à la porte   to kick
  somebody out the door

mettre au courant   to inform
mettre le couvert   to set the table
mettre au point   to make clear
mettre la télé   to turn on the TV
mettre la radio   to turn on the radio

Try reading aloud as fast as you can this play on the sound **mi: Mimi a mis ses amis à Miami.**   Mimi dropped off her friends in Miami.

parler

to talk, to speak

Part. pr. **parlant**   Part. passé **parlé**

The Seven Simple Tenses		The Seven Compound Tenses	
Singular	Plural	Singular	Plural

1 présent de l'indicatif

Singular	Plural
parle	parlons
parles	parlez
parle	parlent

8 passé composé

Singular	Plural
ai parlé	avons parlé
as parlé	avez parlé
a parlé	ont parlé

2 imparfait de l'indicatif

Singular	Plural
parlais	parlions
parlais	parliez
parlait	parlaient

9 plus-que-parfait de l'indicatif

Singular	Plural
avais parlé	avions parlé
avais parlé	aviez parlé
avait parlé	avaient parlé

3 passé simple

Singular	Plural
parlai	parlâmes
parlas	parlâtes
parla	parlèrent

10 passé antérieur

Singular	Plural
eus parlé	eûmes parlé
eus parlé	eûtes parlé
eut parlé	eurent parlé

4 futur

Singular	Plural
parlerai	parlerons
parleras	parlerez
parlera	parleront

11 futur antérieur

Singular	Plural
aurai parlé	aurons parlé
auras parlé	aurez parlé
aura parlé	auront parlé

5 conditionnel

Singular	Plural
parlerais	parlerions
parlerais	parleriez
parlerait	parleraient

12 conditionnel passé

Singular	Plural
aurais parlé	aurions parlé
aurais parlé	auriez parlé
aurait parlé	auraient parlé

6 présent du subjonctif

Singular	Plural
parle	parlions
parles	parliez
parle	parlent

13 passé du subjonctif

Singular	Plural
aie parlé	ayons parlé
aies parlé	ayez parlé
ait parlé	aient parlé

7 imparfait du subjonctif

Singular	Plural
parlasse	parlassions
parlasses	parlassiez
parlât	parlassent

14 plus-que-parfait du subjonctif

Singular	Plural
eusse parlé	eussions parlé
eusses parlé	eussiez parlé
eût parlé	eussent parlé

Impératif
parle
parlons
parlez

Words and expressions related to this verb

parler à haute voix   to speak in a loud voice; **parler haut**   to speak loudly
parler à voix basse   to speak softly; **parler bas**   to speak softly
la parole   spoken word; **parler à**   to talk to; **parler de**   to talk about (of)
selon la parole du Christ   according to Christ's words
le don de la parole   the gift of gab
parler affaires   to talk business, to talk shop
sans parler de. . .   not to mention. . .
parler pour qqn   to speak for someone; **parler contre qqn**   to speak against someone
un parloir   parlor (room where people talk)

prendre

to take

Part. pr. **prenant**   Part. passé **pris**

The Seven Simple Tenses		The Seven Compound Tenses	
Singular	Plural	Singular	Plural
1 présent de l'indicatif		**8 passé composé**	
prends	prenons	ai pris	avons pris
prends	prenez	as pris	avez pris
prend	prennent	a pris	ont pris
2 imparfait de l'indicatif		**9 plus-que-parfait de l'indicatif**	
prenais	prenions	avais pris	avions pris
prenais	preniez	avais pris	aviez pris
prenait	prenaient	avait pris	avaient pris
3 passé simple		**10 passé antérieur**	
pris	prîmes	eus pris	eûmes pris
pris	prîtes	eus pris	eûtes pris
prit	prirent	eut pris	eurent pris
4 futur		**11 futur antérieur**	
prendrai	prendrons	aurai pris	aurons pris
prendras	prendrez	auras pris	aurez pris
prendra	prendront	aura pris	auront pris
5 conditionnel		**12 conditionnel passé**	
prendrais	prendrions	aurais pris	aurions pris
prendrais	prendriez	aurais pris	auriez pris
prendrait	prendraient	aurait pris	auraient pris
6 présent du subjonctif		**13 passé du subjonctif**	
prenne	prenions	aie pris	ayons pris
prennes	preniez	aies pris	ayez pris
prenne	prennent	ait pris	aient pris
7 imparfait du subjonctif		**14 plus-que-parfait du subjonctif**	
prisse	prissions	eusse pris	eussions pris
prisses	prissiez	eusses pris	eussiez pris
prît	prissent	eût pris	eussent pris

Impératif
prends
prenons
prenez

Sentences using this verb and words related to it

—**Qui a pris les fleurs qui étaient sur la table?**
—**C'est moi qui les ai prises.**

à tout prendre   on the whole, all in all
un preneur, une preneuse   taker, purchaser
s'y prendre   to go about it, to handle it, to set about it
Je ne sais comment m'y prendre   I don't know how to go about it.
C'est à prendre ou à laisser   Take it or leave it.
prendre à témoin   to call to witness

rire

to laugh

Part. pr. **riant**   Part. passé **ri**

The Seven Simple Tenses		The Seven Compound Tenses	
Singular	Plural	Singular	Plural

1 présent de l'indicatif

		8 passé composé	
ris	rions	ai ri	avons ri
ris	riez	as ri	avez ri
rit	rient	a ri	ont ri

2 imparfait de l'indicatif

		9 plus-que-parfait de l'indicatif	
riais	riions	avais ri	avions ri
riais	riiez	avais ri	aviez ri
riait	riaient	avait ri	avaient ri

3 passé simple

		10 passé antérieur	
ris	rîmes	eus ri	eûmes ri
ris	rîtes	eus ri	eûtes ri
rit	rirent	eut ri	eurent ri

4 futur

		11 futur antérieur	
rirai	rirons	aurai ri	aurons ri
riras	rirez	auras ri	aurez ri
rira	riront	aura ri	auront ri

5 conditionnel

		12 conditionnel passé	
rirais	ririons	aurais ri	aurions ri
rirais	ririez	aurais ri	auriez ri
rirait	riraient	aurait ri	auraient ri

6 présent du subjonctif

		13 passé du subjonctif	
rie	riions	aie ri	ayons ri
ries	riiez	aies ri	ayez ri
rie	rient	ait ri	aient ri

7 imparfait du subjonctif

		14 plus-que-parfait du subjonctif	
risse	rissions	eusse ri	eussions ri
risses	rissiez	eusses ri	eussiez ri
rit	rissent	eût ri	eussent ri

Impératif
ris
rions
riez

Words and expressions related to this verb

éclater de rire   to burst out laughing; **rire de**   to laugh at
dire qqch pour rire   to say something just for a laugh
rire au nez de qqn   to laugh in someone's face
rire de bon coeur   to laugh heartily
le rire   laughter; **un sourire**   smile; **risible**   laughable

savoir

to know (how)

Part. pr. **sachant**   Part. passé **su**

The Seven Simple Tenses	
Singular	Plural

1 présent de l'indicatif

sais	savons
sais	savez
sait	savent

2 imparfait de l'indicatif

savais	savions
savais	saviez
savait	savaient

3 passé simple

sus	sûmes
sus	sûtes
sut	surent

4 futur

saurai	saurons
sauras	saurez
saura	sauront

5 conditionnel

saurais	saurions
saurais	sauriez
saurait	sauraient

6 présent du subjonctif

sache	sachions
saches	sachiez
sache	sachent

7 imparfait du subjonctif

susse	sussions
susses	sussiez
sût	sussent

The Seven Compound Tenses	
Singular	Plural

8 passé composé

ai su	avons su
as su	avez su
a su	ont su

9 plus-que-parfait de l'indicatif

avais su	avions su
avais su	aviez su
avait su	avaient su

10 passé antérieur

eus su	eûmes su
eus su	eûtes su
eut su	eurent su

11 futur antérieur

aurai su	aurons su
auras su	aurez su
aura su	auront su

12 conditionnel passé

aurais su	aurions su
aurais su	auriez su
aurait su	auraient su

13 passé du subjonctif

aie su	ayons su
aies su	ayez su
ait su	aient su

14 plus-que-parfait du subjonctif

eusse su	eussions su
eusses su	eussiez su
eût su	eussent su

Impératif
sache
sachons
sachez

Words and expressions related to this verb

le savoir   knowledge
le savoir-faire   know-how, tact, ability
le savoir-vivre   to be well-mannered, well-bred
faire savoir   to inform
Pas que je sache   Not to my knowledge

savoir faire qqch   to know how to do something: **Savez-vous jouer du piano?**
Autant que je sache. . .   As far as I know. . .
C'est à savoir   That remains to be seen.

se taire

to be silent, to be quiet, not to speak

Part. pr. **se taisant** Part. passé **tu(e)(s)**

The Seven Simple Tenses		The Seven Compound Tenses	
Singular	Plural	Singular	Plural

1 présent de l'indicatif

me tais	nous taisons	
te tais	vous taisez	
se tait	se taisent	

8 passé composé

me suis tu(e)	nous sommes tu(e)s
t'es tu(e)	vous êtes tu(e)(s)
s'est tu(e)	se sont tu(e)s

2 imparfait de l'indicatif

me taisais	nous taisions
te taisais	vous taisiez
se taisait	se taisaient

9 plus-que-parfait de l'indicatif

m'étais tu(e)	nous étions tu(e)s
t'étais tu(e)	vous étiez tu(e)(s)
s'était tu(e)	s'étaient tu(e)s

3 passé simple

me tus	nous tûmes
te tus	vous tûtes
se tut	se turent

10 passé antérieur

me fus tu(e)	nous fûmes tu(e)s
te fus tu(e)	vous fûtes tu(e)(s)
se fut tu(e)	se furent tu (e)s

4 futur

me tairai	nous tairons
te tairas	vous tairez
se taira	se tairont

11 futur antérieur

me serai tu(e)	nous serons tu(e)s
te seras tu(e)	vous serez tu(e)(s)
se sera tu(e)	se seront tu(e)s

5 conditionnel

me tairais	nous tairions
te tairais	vous tairiez
se tairait	se tairaient

12 conditionnel passé

me serais tu(e)	nous serions tu(e)s
te serais tu(e)	vous seriez tu(e)(s)
se serait tu(e)	se seraient tu(e)s

6 présent du subjonctif

me taise	nous taisions
te taises	vous taisiez
se taise	se taisent

13 passé du subjonctif

me sois tu(e)	nous soyons tu(e)s
te sois tu(e)	vous soyez tu(e)(s)
se soit tu(e)	se soient tu(e)s

7 imparfait du subjonctif

me tusse	nous tussions
te tusses	vous tussiez
se tût	se tussent

14 plus-que-parfait du subjonctif

me fusse tu(e)	nous fussions tu(e)s
te fusses tu(e)	vous fussiez tu(e)(s)
se fût tu(e)	se fussent tu(e)s

Impératif
tais-toi; ne te tais pas
taisons-nous; ne nous taisons pas
taisez-vous; ne vous taisez pas

—**Marie, veux-tu te taire! Tu es trop bavarde. Et toi, Hélène, tais-toi aussi.**
Les deux élèves ne se taisent pas. La maîtresse de chimie continue:
—**Taisez-vous, je vous dis, toutes les deux; autrement, vous resterez dans cette salle après la classe.**
Les deux jeunes filles se sont tues.

vendre

to sell

Part. pr. **vendant**   Part. passé **vendu**

The Seven Simple Tenses		The Seven Compound Tenses	
Singular	Plural	Singular	Plural
1 présent de l'indicatif		**8 passé composé**	
vends	vendons	ai vendu	avons vendu
vends	vendez	as vendu	avez vendu
vend	vendent	a vendu	ont vendu
2 imparfait de l'indicatif		**9 plus-que-parfait de l'indicatif**	
vendais	vendions	avais vendu	avions vendu
vendais	vendiez	avais vendu	aviez vendu
vendait	vendaient	avait vendu	avaient vendu
3 passé simple		**10 passé antérieur**	
vendis	vendîmes	eus vendu	eûmes vendu
vendis	vendîtes	eus vendu	eûtes vendu
vendit	vendirent	eut vendu	eurent vendu
4 futur		**11 futur antérieur**	
vendrai	vendrons	aurai vendu	aurons vendu
vendras	vendrez	auras vendu	aurez vendu
vendra	vendront	aura vendu	auront vendu
5 conditionnel		**12 conditionnel passé**	
vendrais	vendrions	aurais vendu	aurions vendu
vendrais	vendriez	aurais vendu	auriez vendu
vendrait	vendraient	aurait vendu	auraient vendu
6 présent du subjonctif		**13 passé du subjonctif**	
vende	vendions	aie vendu	ayons vendu
vendes	vendiez	aies vendu	ayez vendu
vende	vendent	ait vendu	aient vendu
7 imparfait du subjonctif		**14 plus-que-parfait du subjonctif**	
vendisse	vendissions	eusse vendu	eussions vendu
vendisses	vendissiez	eusses vendu	eussiez vendu
vendît	vendissent	eût vendu	eussent vendu

Impératif
vends
vendons
vendez

Words and expressions related to this verb

un vendeur, une vendeuse salesperson
une vente a sale
maison à vendre house for sale
revendre to resell
en vente on sale
une salle de vente sales room

vendre à bon marché to sell at a reasonably low price (a good buy)
une vente aux enchères auction sale
vendre au rabais to sell at a discount
On vend des livres ici Books are sold here.

vouloir

to want

Part. pr. **voulant**   Part. passé **voulu**

The Seven Simple Tenses		The Seven Compound Tenses	
Singular	Plural	Singular	Plural
1 présent de l'indicatif		**8 passé composé**	
veux	voulons	ai voulu	avons voulu
veux	voulez	as voulu	avez voulu
veut	veulent	a voulu	ont voulu
2 imparfait de l'indicatif		**9 plus-que-parfait de l'indicatif**	
voulais	voulions	avais voulu	avions voulu
voulais	vouliez	avais voulu	aviez voulu
voulait	voulaient	avait voulu	avaient voulu
3 passé simple		**10 passé antérieur**	
voulus	voulûmes	eus voulu	eûmes voulu
voulus	voulûtes	eus voulu	eûtes voulu
voulut	voulurent	eut voulu	eurent voulu
4 futur		**11 futur antérieur**	
voudrai	voudrons	aurai voulu	aurons voulu
voudras	voudrez	auras voulu	aurez voulu
voudra	voudront	aura voulu	auront voulu
5 conditionnel		**12 conditionnel passé**	
voudrais	voudrions	aurais voulu	aurions voulu
voudrais	voudriez	aurais voulu	auriez voulu
voudrait	voudraient	aurait voulu	auraient voulu
6 présent du subjonctif		**13 passé du subjonctif**	
veuille	voulions	aie voulu	ayons voulu
veuilles	vouliez	aies voulu	ayez voulu
veuille	veuillent	ait voulu	aient voulu
7 imparfait du subjonctif		**14 plus-que-parfait du subjonctif**	
voulusse	voulussions	eusse voulu	eussions voulu
voulusses	voulussiez	eusses voulu	eussiez voulu
voulût	voulussent	eût voulu	eussent voulu

Impératif
veuille
veuillons
veuillez

Words and expressions related to this verb

un voeu   a wish
meilleurs voeux   best wishes
Vouloir c'est pouvoir   Where there's a will there's a way.
vouloir dire   to mean; **Qu'est-ce que cela veut dire?** What does that mean?
vouloir bien faire qqch   to be willing to do something

sans le vouloir   without meaning to, unintentionally
en temps voulu   in due time
en vouloir à qqn   to bear a grudge against someone
Que voulez-vous dire par là?   What do you mean by that remark?

Review of basic French idioms
with aller, avoir, être, faire

With aller

aller, to feel (health); **Comment allez-vous?**
aller à la rencontre de quelqu'un, to go to meet someone
aller à pied, to walk, to go on foot
aller chercher, to go get
allons donc! nonsense! come on, now!
s'en aller, to go away

With avoir

avoir . . . ans, to be . . . years old; **Quel âge avez-vous? J'ai dix-sept ans.**
avoir à + inf., to have to, to be obliged to + inf.
avoir affaire à quelqu'un, to deal with someone
avoir beau + inf., to be useless + inf., to do something in vain; **Vous avez beau parler; je ne vous écoute pas,** You are talking in vain; I am not listening to you.
avoir besoin de, to need, to have need of
avoir bonne mine, to look well, to look good (persons)
avoir chaud, to be (feel) warm (persons)
avoir congé, to have a day off, a holiday
avoir de la chance, to be lucky
avoir envie de + inf., to feel like, to have a desire to
avoir faim, to be (feel) hungry
avoir froid, to be (feel) cold (persons)
avoir hâte, to be in a hurry
avoir honte, to be ashamed, to feel ashamed
avoir l'air + adj., to seem, to appear, to look + adj.; **Vous avez l'air malade,** You look sick.
avoir l'air de + inf., to appear + inf.; **Vous avez l'air d'être malade,** You appear to be sick.
avoir l'habitude de + inf., to be accustomed to, to be in the habit of; **J'ai l'habitude de faire mes devoirs avant le dîner,** I'm in the habit of doing my homework before dinner.
avoir l'idée de + inf., to have a notion + inf.
avoir l'intention de + inf., to intend + inf.
avoir la bonté de + inf., to have the kindness + inf.
avoir la parole, to have the floor (to speak)

avoir le temps de + inf., to have (the) time + inf.
avoir lieu, to take place
avoir mal, to feel sick
avoir mal à + (place where it hurts), to have a pain or ache in . . . ; **J'ai mal à la jambe,** My leg hurts
avoir mauvaise mine, to look ill, not to look
avoir peine à + inf., to have difficulty in + pres. part.
avoir peur de, to be afraid of
avoir raison, to be right (persons)
avoir soif, to be thirsty
avoir sommeil, to be sleepy
avoir tort, to be wrong (persons)

With être

être à l'heure, to be on time
être à quelqu'un, to belong to someone; **Ce livre est à moi,** This book belongs to me.
être à temps, to be in time
être au courant de, to be informed about
être bien, to be comfortable
être bien aise (de), to be very glad, happy (to)
être d'accord avec, to agree with
être de retour, to be back
être en état de + inf., to be able + inf.
être en retard, to be late, not to be on time
être en train de + inf., to be in the act of + pres. part., to be in the process of, to be busy + pres. part.
être en vacances, to be on vacation
être enrhumé, to have a cold, to be sick with a cold
être le bienvenu (la bienvenue), to be welcomed
être pressé(e), to be in a hurry
être sur le point de + inf., to be about + inf.
être temps de + inf., to be time + inf.
Quelle heure est-il? What time is it? **Il est une heure,** It is one o'clock; **Il est deux heures,** It is two o'clock.
y être, to be there, to understand it, to get it; **J'y suis!** I get it! I understand it!

Il était une fois . . . , Once upon a time there was (there were) . . .

With faire

Cela ne fait rien, That doesn't matter, That makes no difference.

Comment se fait-il? How come?

en faire autant, to do the same, to do as much

faire + inf., to have something done

faire à sa tête, to have one's way

faire attention (à), to pay attention (to)

faire beau, to be pleasant, nice weather

faire bon accueil, to welcome

faire chaud, to be warm (weather)

faire de son mieux, to do one's best

faire des emplettes; faire des courses; faire du shopping, to do or to go shopping

faire des progrès, to make progress

faire du bien à quelqu'un, to do good for someone; **Cela lui fera du bien,** That will do her (or him) some good.

faire face à, to oppose

faire faire quelque chose, to have something done or made; **Je me fais faire une robe** / I'm having a dress made (by someone) for myself.

faire froid, to be cold (weather)

faire jour, to be daylight

faire la connaissance de quelqu'un, to make the acquaintance of someone, to meet someone for the first time, to become acquainted with someone

faire la cuisine, to do the cooking

faire la queue, to line up, to get in line, to stand in line, to queue up

faire le ménage, to do housework

faire le tour de, to take a stroll, to go around

faire mal à quelqu'un, to hurt, to harm someone

faire nuit, to be night(time)

faire part à quelqu'un, to inform someone

faire part de quelque chose à quelqu'un, to let someone know about something, to inform, to notify someone of something

faire partie de, to be a part of

faire peur à quelqu'un, to frighten someone

faire plaisir à quelqu'un, to please someone

faire savoir quelque chose à quelqu'un, to inform someone of something

faire semblant de + inf., to pretend + inf.

faire ses adieux, to say good-bye

faire son possible, to do one's best

faire un tour, to go for a stroll

faire un voyage, to take a trip

faire une partie de, to play a game of

faire une promenade, to take a walk

faire une promenade en voiture, to go for a drive

faire une question, to ask, to pose a question

faire une visite, to pay a visit

faire venir quelqu'un, to have someone come; **Il a fait venir le docteur,** He had the doctor come.

Faites comme chez vous! Make yourself at home!

Que faire? What is to be done?

Quel temps fait-il? What's the weather like?

Numbers

Cardinal Numbers: 1 to 1,000

0 zéro	31 trente et un	201 deux cent un
1 un, une	32 trente-deux, *etc.*	202 deux cent deux, etc.
2 deux	**40 quarante**	**300 trois cents**
3 trois	41 quarante et un	301 trois cent un
4 quatre	42 quarante-deux, *etc.*	302 trois cent deux, *etc.*
5 cinq	**50 cinquante**	**400 quatre cents**
6 six	51 cinquante et un	401 quatre cent un
7 sept	52 cinquante-deux, *etc.*	402 quatre cent deux, *etc.*
8 huit	**60 soixante**	**500 cinq cents**
9 neuf	61 soixante et un	501 cinq cent un
10 dix	62 soixante-deux, *etc.*	502 cinq cent deux, *etc.*
11 onze	**70 soixante-dix**	**600 six cents**
12 douze	71 soixante et onze	601 six cent un
13 treize	72 soixante-douze, *etc.*	602 six cent deux, *etc.*
14 quatorze	**80 quatre-vingts**	**700 sept cents**
15 quinze	81 quatre-vingt-un	701 sept cent un
16 seize	82 quatre-vingt-deux, *etc.*	702 sept cent deux, *etc.*
17 dix-sept	**90 quatre-vingt-dix**	**800 huit cents**
18 dix-huit	91 quatre-vingt-onze	801 huit cent un
19 dix-neuf	92 quatre-vingt-douze, *etc.*	802 huit cent deux, *etc.*
20 vingt	**100 cent**	**900 neuf cents**
21 vingt et un	101 cent un	901 neuf cent un
22 vingt-deux, *etc.*	102 cent deux, *etc.*	902 neuf cent deux, *etc.*
30 trente	**200 deux cents**	**1,000 mille**

Ordinal numbers: first to twentieth

first	**premier, première**	1st	**1er, 1re**
second	**deuxième (second, seconde)**	2d	**2e**
third	**troisième**	3d	**3e**
fourth	**quatrième**	4th	**4e**
fifth	**cinquième**	5th	**5e**
sixth	**sixième**	6th	**6e**
seventh	**septième**	7th	**7e**
eighth	**huitième**	8th	**8e**
ninth	**neuvième**	9th	**9e**
tenth	**dixième**	10th	**10e**
eleventh	**onzième**	11th	**11e**
twelfth	**douzième**	12th	**12e**
thirteenth	**treizième**	13th	**13e**
fourteenth	**quatorzième**	14th	**14e**
fifteenth	**quinzième**	15th	**15e**
sixteenth	**seizième**	16th	**16e**
seventeenth	**dix-septième**	17th	**17e**
eighteenth	**dix-huitième**	18th	**18e**
nineteenth	**dix-neuvième**	19th	**19e**
twentieth	**vingtième**	20th	**20e**

Antonyms and synonyms

An antonym is a word that has the opposite meaning of another word. A synonym is a word that has the same or similar meaning as another word.

Antonyms

absent, absente *adj.*, absent	**présent, présente** *adj.*, present
acheter *v.*, to buy	**vendre** *v.*, to sell
agréable *adj.*, pleasant, agreeable	**désagréable** *adj.*, unpleasant, disagreeable
aimable *adj.*, kind	**méchant, méchante** *adj.*, mean, nasty
ami, amie *n.*, friend	**ennemi, ennemie** *n.*, enemy
beau, belle *adj.*, beautiful, handsome	**laid, laide** *adj.*, ugly
beaucoup (de) *adv.*, much, many	**peu (de)** *adv.*, little, some
beauté *n. f.*, beauty	**laideur** *n. f.*, ugliness
bête *adj.*, stupid	**intelligent, intelligente** *adj.*, intelligent
blanc, blanche *adj.*, white	**noir, noire** *adj.*, black
bon, bonne *adj.*, good	**mauvais, mauvaise** *adj.*, bad
bonheur *n. m.*, happiness	**malheur** *n. m.*, unhappiness
chaud, chaude *adj.*, hot, warm	**froid, froide** *adj.*, cold
content, contente *adj.*, glad, pleased	**mécontent, mécontente** *adj.*, displeased
court, courte *adj.*, short	**long, longue** *adj.*, long
dedans *adv.*, inside	**dehors** *adv.*, outside
dernier, dernière *adj.*, last	**premier, première** *adj.*, first
derrière *adv., prep.*, behind	**devant** *adv., prep.*, in front of
dessous *adv., prep.*, below, underneath	**dessus** *adv., prep.*, above, over
différent, différente *adj.*, different	**même** *adj.*, same
difficile *adj.*, difficult	**facile** *adj.*, easy
domestique *adj.*, domestic	**sauvage** *adj.*, wild
donner *v.*, to give	**recevoir** *v.*, to receive
étroit, étroite *adj.*, narrow	**large** *adj.*, wide
faible *adj.*, weak	**fort, forte** *adj.*, strong
fin *n. f.*, end	**commencement** *n. m.*, beginning
finir *v.*, to finish	**commencer** *v.*, to begin
gai, gaie *adj.*, gay, happy	**triste** *adj.*, sad
grand, grande *adj.*, large, tall, big	**petit, petite** *adj.*, small, little
gros, grosse *adj.*, fat	**maigre** *adj.*, thin
heureux, heureuse *adj.*, happy	**malheureux, malheureuse** *adj.*, unhappy
homme *n. m.*, man	**femme** *n. f.*, woman
inutile *adj.*, useless	**utile** *adj.*, useful
jamais *adv.*, never	**toujours** *adv.*, always
jeune *adj.*, young	**vieux, vieille** *adj.*, old
jeune fille *n. f.*, girl	**garçon** *n. m.*, boy
joli, jolie *adj.*, pretty	**laid, laide** *adj.*, ugly
jour *n. m.*, day	**nuit** *n. f.*, night
lentement *adv.*, slowly	**vite** *adv.*, quickly
mal *adv.*, badly	**bien** *adv.*, well
moins *adv.*, less	**plus** *adv.*, more
oui *adv.*, yes	**non** *adv.*, no

paix *n. f.*, peace	**guerre** *n. f.*, war
partir *v.*, to leave	**arriver** *v.*, to arrive
pauvre *adj.*, poor	**riche** *adj.*, rich
plein, pleine *adj.*, full	**vide** *adj.*, empty
question *n. f.*, question	**réponse** *n. f.*, answer, reply, response
refuser *v.*, to refuse	**accepter** *v.*, to accept
rire *v.*, to laugh	**pleurer** *v.*, to cry, to weep
sans *prep.*, without	**avec** *prep.*, with
silence *n. m.*, silence	**bruit** *n. m.*, noise
sûr, sûre *adj.*, sure, certain	**incertain, incertaine** *adj.*, unsure
tôt *adv.*, early	**tard** *adv.*, late
travailler *v.*, to work	**jouer** *v.*, to play

Synonyms

aimer mieux *v.*, **préférer**	to prefer
auteur *n. m.*, **écrivain**	author, writer
bâtiment *n. m.*, **édifice**	building, edifice
certain, certaine *adj.*, **sûr, sûre**	certain, sure
content, contente *adj.*, **heureux, heureuse**	content, happy
docteur *n. m.*, **médecin**	doctor, physician
erreur *n. f.*, **faute**	error, mistake
façon *n. f.*, **manière**	manner, way
fameux, fameuse *adj.*, **célèbre**	famous
favori, favorite *adj.*, **préféré, préférée**	favorite, preferred
femme *n. f.*, **épouse**	wife, spouse
finir *v.*, **terminer**	to finish, end, terminate
glace *n. f.*, **le miroir**	mirror
habiter *v.*, **demeurer**	to live (in), dwell, inhabit
image *n. f.*, **le tableau**	picture
lieu *n. m.*, **endroit**	place
maître, *n. m.*, **instituteur**	teacher (man)
maîtresse *n. f.*, **institutrice**	teacher (woman)
mari *n. m.*, **époux**	husband, spouse
pays *n. m.*, **la nation**	country, nation
rester *v.*, **demeurer**	to stay, to remain
sérieux, sérieuse *adj.*, **grave**	serious, grave
tout de suite *adv.*, **immédiatement**	right away, immediately
triste *adj.*, **malheureux, malheureuse**	sad, unhappy
vêtements *n. m.*, **habits**	clothes, clothing
vite *adv.*, **rapidement**	quickly, fast, rapidly

Review of
Basic Vocabulary by Topics

◆

L'École
(School)

banc *n. m.*, seat, bench

bibliothèque *n. f.*, library

bureau *n. m.*, desk, office

cahier *n. m.*, notebook

calendrier *n. m.*, calendar

carnet *n. m.*, small notebook

carte *n. f.*, map

classe *n. f.*, class; **la classe de français** French class

congé *n. m.*, leave, permission; **jour de congé** day off (from school or work)

cour *n. f.*, playground, courtyard

craie *n. f.*, chalk

crayon *n. m.*, pencil; **le crayon feutre** the crayon

devoirs *n. m.*, *pl.*, homework assignments

dictée *n. f.*, dictation

drapeau *n. m.*, flag

echouer *v.*, to fail

echouer à un examen to fail an exam

école *n. f.*, school

écrire *v.*, to write

élève *n. m. f.*, pupil

encre *n. f.*, ink

étudier *v.*, to study; **les études** *n. f. pl.*, the studies

étudiant *m.*, étudiante *f.*, *n.*, student

examen *n. m.*, examination

exercice *n. m.*, exercise

expliquer *v.*, to explain

faute *n. f.*, mistake

leçon *n. f.*, lesson; **leçon de français** French lesson

livre *n. m.*, book

livret d'exercices *n. m.*, workbook

lycée *n. m.*, high school

maître *m.*, maîtresse *f.*, *n.*, teacher

papier *n. m.*, paper; **une feuille de papier** a sheet of paper

passer *v.*, to pass; **passer un examen** to take an exam

poser *v.*, to pose; **poser une question** to ask a question

professeur *m.*, **professeur-dame, une femme professeur** *f.*, *n.*, professor

pupitre *n. m.*, desk (student's)

règle *n. f.*, rule, ruler

répondre *v.*, to respond, to answer, to reply

réponse *n. f.*, answer

réussir *v.*, to succeed; **réussir à un examen** to pass an exam

salle *n. f.*, room; **la salle de classe** the classroom

stylo *n. m.*, pen

tableau noir *n. m.*, blackboard, chalkboard

université *n. f.*, university

vocabulaire *n. m.*, vocabulary

Les Jours de la semaine, les mois de l'année, les saisons, et les jours de fête

(Days of the Week, Months of the Year, Seasons, and Holidays)

Les jours de la semaine

le dimanche, Sunday
le lundi, Monday
le mardi, Tuesday
le mercredi, Wednesday
le jeudi, Thursday
le vendredi, Friday
le samedi, Saturday

Les saisons

le printemps, spring
l'été *m.,* summer
l'automne *m.,* autumn, fall
l'hiver *m.,* winter

Les mois de l'année

janvier, January
février, February
mars, March
avril, April
mai, May
juin, June
juillet, July
août, August
septembre, September
octobre, October
novembre, November
décembre, December

Les jours de fête

fêter *v.,* to celebrate a holiday; **bonne fête!** happy holiday!
l'anniversaire *m.,* anniversary, birthday; **bon anniversaire!** happy anniversary! *or* happy birthday!
le Jour de l'An, New Year's Day
Bonne Année! Happy New Year!
les Pâques, Easter; **Joyeuses Pâques,** Happy Easter
la Pâque, Passover
le quatorze juillet (Bastille Day), July 14, French "Independence Day"
les grandes vacances, summer vacation
la Toussaint, All Saints' Day (le premier novembre)
le Noël, Christmas; **Joyeux Noël!** Merry Christmas!
à vous de même! the same to you!

Les légumes, les poissons, les viandes, les produits laitiers, les desserts, les fromages et les boissons

(Vegetables, Fish, Meats, Dairy Products, Desserts, Cheeses, and Beverages)

Les légumes

aubergine *f.*, eggplant
carotte *f.*, carrot
champignon *m.*, mushroom
épinards *m. pl.*, spinach
haricots verts *m. pl.*, string beans
maïs *m.*, corn
oignon *m.*, onion
petits pois *m. pl.*, peas
pomme de terre *f.*, potato

Les viandes

agneau *m.*, lamb; **la côte d'agneau**, lamb chop
biftek *m.*, steak
jambon, *m.*, ham
porc *m.*, pork
poulet, *m.*, chicken
rosbif *m.*, roast beef
veau *m.*, veal; **la côte de veau**, veal chop

Les poissons

maquereau *m.*, mackerel
morue *f.*, cod
saumon *m.*, salmon
sole *f.*, sole
truite *f.*, trout

Les produits laitiers

beurre *m.*, butter
crème *f.*, cream
fromage *m.*, cheese
lait *m.*, milk
oeuf *m.*, egg

Les desserts

fruit *m.*, fruit
gâteau *m.*, cake; **le gâteau sec**, cookie
glace *f.*, ice cream
pâtisserie *f.*, pastry

Les fromages

brie *m.*
camembert *m.*
gruyère *m.*
petit suisse *m.*
port-salut *m.*
roquefort *m.*

Les boissons

bière *f.*, beer
cacao *m.*, cocoa
café *m.*, coffee
chocolat chaud *m.*, hot chocolate
cidre *m.*, cider
eau minérale *f.*, mineral water
jus *m.*, juice; **le jus de tomate**, tomato juice
thé *m.*, tea
vin *m.*, wine

Les animaux, les fleurs, les couleurs, les arbres et les fruits
(Animals, Flowers, Colors, Trees, and Fruits)

Les animaux

âne *m.*, donkey
chat *m.*, **chatte** *f.*, cat
cheval *m.*, horse
chien *m.*, **chienne** *f.*, dog
cochon *m.*, pig
coq *m.*, rooster
éléphant *m.*, elephant
lapin *m.*, rabbit
lion *m.*, lion
oiseau *m.*, bird
poule *f.*, hen
poulet *m.*, chicken
renard *m.*, fox
souris *f.*, mouse
tigre *m.*, tiger
vache *f.*, cow

Les fleurs

iris *m.*, iris
lilas m., lilac
lis *m.*, lily
marguerite *f.*, daisy
oeillet *m.*, carnation
rose *f.*, rose
tulipe *f.*, tulip
violette *f.*, violet

Les couleurs
(all are masculine)

blanc, white
bleu, blue
brun, brown
gris, gray
jaune, yellow
noir, black
rouge, red
vert, green

Les arbres

bananier *m.*, banana tree
cerisier *m.*, cherry tree
citronnier *m.*, lemon tree
oranger *m.*, orange tree
palmier *m.*, palm tree
pêcher *m.*, peach tree
poirier *m.*, pear tree
pommier *m.*, apple tree

Les fruits

banane *f.*, banana
cerise *f.*, cherry
citron *m.*, lemon; **citron vert,** lime
fraise *f.*, strawberry
framboise *f.*, raspberry
orange *f.*, orange
pamplemousse *m.*, grapefruit
pêche *f.*, peach
poire *f.*, pear
pomme *f.*, apple
raisin *m.*, grape
tomate *f.*, tomato

Le corps humain, les vêtements, la toilette

(The Human Body, Clothing, Washing and Dressing)

Le corps humain

bouche *f.*, mouth
bras *m.*, arm
cheveux *m. pl.*, hair
cou *m.*, neck
dents *f. pl.*, teeth
doigt *m.*, finger; **doigt de pied,** toe
épaule *f.*, shoulder
estomac *m.*, stomach
genou *m.*, knee
jambe *f.*, leg
langue *f.*, tongue
lèvres *f. pl.*, lips
main *f.*, hand
menton *m.*, chin
nez *m.*, nose
oeil *m.*, eye; **les yeux,** eyes
oreille *f.*, ear
peau *f.*, skin
pied *m.*, foot
poitrine *f.*, chest
tête *f.*, head
visage *m.*, face

La toilette

se baigner *v.*, to bathe oneself
baignoire *n. f.*, bathtub
bain *n. m.*, bath
brosse *n. f.*, brush; **brosse à dents,** toothbrush
brosser *v.*, to brush; **se brosser les dents,** to brush one's teeth
cuvette *n. f.*, toilet bowl
dentifrice *n. m.*, toothpaste
déodorant *n. m.*, deodorant
déshabiller *v.*, to undress; **se déshabiller,** to undress oneself
douche *n. f.*, shower; **prendre une douche,** to take a shower
enlever *v.*, to remove, to take off
gant de toilette *n. m.*, washcloth
glace *n. f.*, hand mirror
s'habiller *v.*, to dress oneself
lavabo *n. m.*, washroom, washstand
laver *v.*, to wash; **se laver,** to wash oneself
mettre *v.*, to put on
miroir *n. m.*, mirror
ôter *v.*, to take off, to remove
peigne *n. m.*, comb; **se peigner les cheveux,** to comb one's hair
porter *v.*, to wear
salle de bains *n. f.*, bathroom
savon *n. m.*, soap
serviette *n. f.*, towel
shampooing *n. m.*, shampoo

Les vêtements

bas, *m.*, stocking
béret *m.*, beret
blouse *f.*, blouse, smock
blouson *m.*, jacket (often with zipper)
chandail *m.*, sweater
chapeau *m.*, hat
chaussette *f.*, sock
chaussure *f.*, shoe
chemise *f.*, shirt
complet *m.*, suit
costume *m.*, suit
cravate *f.*, necktie
écharpe *f.*, scarf
gant *m.*, glove
jupe *f.*, skirt
maillot de bain *m.*, swim suit
manteau *m.*, coat
pantalon *m.*, trousers, pants
pantoufle *f.*, slipper
pardessus *m.*, overcoat
poche *f.*, pocket
pullover *m.*, pullover or long-sleeved sweater
robe *f.*, dress
soulier *m.*, shoe
veston *m.*, (suit) coat

La famille, la maison, les meubles
(Family, Home, Furniture)

La famille

cousin *m.*, **cousine** *f.*, cousin
enfant *m. f.*, child
époux *m.*, **épouse** *f.*, spouse
  (husband/wife)
femme *f.*, wife
fille *f.*, daughter
fils *m.*, son
frère *m.*, brother; **le**
  beau-frère, brother-in-law
grand-mère *f.*, grandmother
grand-père *m.*, grandfather
les grands-parents *m.*,
  grandparents
mari *m.*, husband
mère, maman *f.*, mother; **la**
  belle-mère, mother-in-law
neveu *m.*, nephew
nièce *f.*, niece
oncle *m.*, uncle
père, papa *m.*, father; **le**
  beau-père, father-in-law
petit-fils *m.*, grandson
petite-fille *f.*, granddaughter
petits-enfants *m. pl.*,
  grandchildren
soeur *f.*, sister; **la belle-soeur**,
  sister-in-law
tante *f.*, aunt

La maison

cave *f.*, cellar
chambre *f.*, room; **chambre à**
  coucher, bedroom
cheminée *f.*, fireplace, chimney
cuisine *f.*, kitchen
escalier *m.*, stairs, staircase
fenêtre *f.*, window
mur *m.*, wall
pièce *f.*, room
plafond *m.*, ceiling
plancher *m.*, floor
porte *f.*, door
salle *f.*, room; **la salle à**
  manger, dining room; **la**
  salle de bains, bathroom
salon *m.*, living room
toit *m.*, roof

Les meubles

armoire *f.*, wardrobe closet
bureau *m.*, desk
canapé *m.*, sofa, couch
chaise *f.*, chair
commode *f.*, dresser, chest of
  drawers
couchette *f.*, bunk
évier *m.*, kitchen sink
fauteuil *m.*, armchair
four *m.*, oven
fournaise *f.*, furnace
fourneau *m.*, kitchen stove,
  range
lampe *f.*, lamp
lit *m.*, bed
phonographe *m.*, phonograph
piano *m.*, piano
radio stéréophonique *f.*,
  stereophonic radio
table *f.*, table
tapis *m.*, carpet
téléphone *m.*, telephone
téléviseur *m.*, television (set)

La ville, les bâtiments, les magasins, les divers modes de transport
(The City, Buildings, Stores, Various Means of Transportation)

La ville

avenue *f.,* avenue
boîte aux lettres *f.,* mailbox
bouche de métro *f.,* subway entrance
boulevard *m.,* boulevard
bruit *m.,* noise
chaussée *f.,* road
défense d'afficher, post no bills
feux *m. pl.,* traffic lights
parc *m.,* park
pollution *f.,* pollution
rue *f.,* street
trottoir *m.,* sidewalk
voiture de police *f.,* police car

Les bâtiments

banque *f.,* bank
bibliothèque *f.,* library
bureau de poste *m.,* post office
cathédrale *f.,* cathedral
chapelle *f.,* chapel
château *m.,* castle
cinéma *m.,* movie theater
école *f.,* school
église *f.,* church
gare *f.,* railroad station
grange *f.,* barn
gratte-ciel *m.,* skyscraper
hôpital *m.,* hospital
hôtel *m.,* hotel
hôtel de ville *m.,* city hall
hutte *f.,* hut, cabin
immeuble d'habitation *m.,* apartment building
musée *m.,* museum
palais *m.,* palace
synagogue *f.,* synagogue
temple *m.,* temple
théâtre *m.,* theater
usine *f.,* factory

Les magasins

bijouterie *f.,* jewelry shop
blanchisserie *f.,* laundry
boucherie *f.,* butcher shop
boulangerie *f.,* bakery (mostly for bread)
boutique *f.,* (small) shop
bureau de tabac *m.,* tobacco shop
café *m.,* café
charcuterie *f.,* pork store, delicatessen
crémerie *f.,* dairy store
épicerie *f.,* grocery store
grand magasin *m.,* department store
librairie *f.,* bookstore
magasin *m.,* store
pâtisserie *f.,* pastry shop
pharmacie *f.,* drugstore
supermarché *m.,* supermarket

Les divers modes de transport

autobus *m.,* city bus
autocar *m.,* interurban bus
automobile *f.,* car
avion *m.,* plane
bateau *m.,* boat
bicyclette *f.,* bicycle
camion *m.,* truck
chemin de fer *m.,* railroad
métro *m.,* subway
moto *f.,* motorcycle
train *m.,* train
transatlantique *m.,* ocean liner
vélo *m.,* bike
voiture *f.,* car

Les métiers et les professions, les langues, pays et les continents

(Trades and Professions, Languages, Countries, and Continents)

Les métiers et les professions

acteur *m.*, **actrice** *f.*, actor, actress
agent de police *m.*, police officer
auteur *m.*, author (of a book) *or* composer (of a song) *or* painter (of a picture)
avocat *m.*, **la femme-avocat** *f.*, lawyer
bijoutier *m.*, **bijoutière** f., jeweler
blanchisseur *m.*, **blanchisseuse** *f.*, launderer
boucher *m.*, **bouchère** *f.*, butcher
boulanger *m.*, **boulangère** *f.*, baker
charcutier *m.*, **charcutière** *f.*, pork butcher
chauffeur *m.*, driver, chauffeur
coiffeur *m.*, **coiffeuse** *f.*, hairdresser, barber
dentiste *m.*, *f.*, dentist
épicier *m.*, **épicière** *f.*, grocer
facteur *m.*, letter carrier
fermier *m.*, **fermière** *f.*, farmer
libraire *m.*, *f.*, bookseller
maître *m.*, **maîtresse** *f.*, teacher
marchand *m.*, **marchande** *f.*, merchant
médecin *m.*, **femme-médecin** *f.*, doctor
pâtissier *m.*, **pâtissière** *f.*, pastry chef
pharmacien *m.*, **pharmacienne** *f.*, pharmacist
professeur *m.*, **femme-professeur** *f.*, professor
sénateur *m.*, senator
serveur *m.*, **serveuse** *f.*, waiter, waitress
tailleur *m.*, **tailleuse** *f.*, tailor
vendeur *m.*, **vendeuse** *f.*, salesperson

Les langues (all are masculine)

allemand, German
anglais, English
chinois, Chinese
danois, Danish
espagnol, Spanish; **castillan,** Castilian (Spanish)
français, French
grec ancien, Ancient Greek
grec moderne, Modern Greek
hébreu, Hebrew
italien, Italian
japonais, Japanese
latin, Latin
norvégien, Norwegian
portugais, Portuguese
russe, Russian
suédois Swedish

Les pays, les continents

l'Allemagne *f.*, Germany
l'Angleterre *f.*, England
l'Australie *f.*, Australia
la Belgique, Belgium
le Canada, Canada
la Chine, China
le Danemark, Denmark
l'Espagne *f.*, Spain
les États-Unis *m.*, United States
l'Europe *f.*, Europe
la France, France
la Grande-Bretagne, Great Britain
la Grèce, Greece
la Hollande, Holland
l'Irlande *f.*, Ireland
l'Israël *m.*, Israel
l'Italie *f.*, Italy
le Japon, Japan
le Luxembourg, Luxembourg
le Mexique, Mexico
la Norvège, Norway
la Pologne, Poland
le Porto Rico, Puerto Rico
le Portugal, Portugal
la Russie, Russia; **U.R.S.S.,** Union des Républiques Socialistes Soviétiques (U.S.S.R.)
la Suède, Sweden
la Suisse, Switzerland

Vocabulary
French and English Words
in one alphabetical listing

◆

This list of vocabulary contains words and expressions in French and English in one alphabetical order for convenience. One listing prevents you from looking inadvertently in a French listing for an English word or in an English listing for a French word. Also, cognates and near-cognates in both languages are reduced to a single entry. All French words are printed in bold face.

The preposition *to* in an English infinitive is omitted, e.g., *to go* is listed under *go*.

If you do not understand the meaning of an abbreviation, look it up in the list of abbreviations here below.

Entries in this vocabulary pertain to words used in this book. For any not listed here, consult a standard French-English/English-French dictionary.

Abbreviations

adj.	adjective	*fam.*	familiar	*par.*	paragraph
adv.	adverb	*fut.*	future	*part.*	participle
advl.	adverbial	*i.e.*	that is, that is to say	*per.*	personal
art.	article	*illus.*	illustration	*pers.*	person
cond.	conditional	*indef.*	indefinite	*pl.*	plural
conj.	conjunction	*indic.*	indicative	*poss.*	possessive
def.	definite	*indir.*	indirect	*prep.*	preposition
dem.	demonstrative	*inf.*	infinitive	*pres.*	present
dir.	direct	*interj.*	interjection	*pron.*	pronoun
disj.	disjunctive	*interrog.*	interrogative	*refl.*	reflexive
e.g.	for example	*m.* or *masc.*	masculine	*rel.*	relative
etc.	et cetera, and so on	*n.*	noun	*s.* or *sing.*	singular
exclam.	exclamation	*no.*	number	*subj.*	subject
expr.	expression	*obj.*	object	*v.*	verb
f. or *fem.*	feminine	*p.*	page		

A

à *prep.*, at, to; **à l'heure** on time; **à quelle heure?** at what time?

accepter *v.*, to accept; *past part.* **accepté; je ne peux pas accepter** I can't accept

acheter *v.*, to buy, to purchase; *past part.*, **acheté**

actor *n.*, **un acteur**; actress, **une actrice**

adresse *n.f.*, address

afraid, to be *v.*, **avoir peur**; see the verb **avoir** and the review of basic French idioms with **avoir** in the Appendix

afternoon *n.*, **un après-midi**

ai *pres. indic., 1st pers., sing. of* **avoir; j'ai,** I have; see the verb **avoir** in the Appendix

aimer *v.*, to like, to love; **vous aimez** you like (love); **aimez-vous?** do you like?

air *n.m.*, air; tune (music)

alarm clock *n.*, **le réveil**

aller *v.*, to go; *past part.* **allé; je suis allé(e),** I went (I did go, I have gone); **allez-vous?** are you going? (do you go?); see also the verb **aller** and the review of basic French idioms with **aller** in the Appendix

allô *exclam.*, hello (used when answering a telephone)

ami(e) *n.m. (f.)*, friend

amitié *n.f.*, friendship

amusing *adj.*, **amusant(e)**

an *n.m.*, year

and *conj.*, **et**

angry *adj.*, **fâché(e)**

animaux *n.m., pl.*, animals

answer *v.*, **répondre**; *past part.* **répondu;** *n.*, **la réponse**

apprendre *v.*, to learn; *past part.* **appris**

après-midi *n.m.* afternoon

are there . . . ? **y a-t-il . . . ?**

arriver *v.*, to arrive; *past part.* **arrrivé; je suis arrivé(e),** I arrived (I did arrive, I have arrived); **l'arrivée** *n.f.*, arrival

s'asseoir *refl. v.*, to sit down; see the verb **s'asseoir** in the Appendix

assez *adv.*, enough

assignment, *n.*, **le devoir**

assister (à) *v.*, to be present at, to assist; *past part.* **assisté**

at *prep.*, **à**; at the same time as, **en même temps que;** at what time? **à quelle heure?**

au cinéma, to (at) the movies; **au théâtre,** to (at) the theater

audience, *n.*, **les spectateurs**

automne *n.m.*, autumn, fall; see the seasons of the year in the Appendix

avec *prep.*, with

avoir *v.*, to have; *past part.* **eu; j'ai eu un bon petit déjeuner,** I had a good breakfast; **avoir tort,** to be mistaken; **avoir raison,** to be right; **avez-vous . . . ?** have you . . . ? do you have . . . ? see also the verb **avoir** and the review of basic French idioms with **avoir** in the Appendix

B

bain *n.m.*, bath; **une salle de bains,** bathroom

ball *n.*, **une balle**; large ball, **un ballon**; to play ball, **jouer à la balle**

basketball *n.*, **le basket-ball**

be *v.*, **être**; *past part.* **été**; see the verb **être** in the Appendix

beach, *n.*, **la plage**

beaucoup *adv.*, much, many

beautiful *adj.*, **beau, bel, belle, beaux, belles; un beau livre, un bel arbre, une belle maison, de beaux livres, de belles maisons**

because *conj.*, **parce que**

bed, *n.*, **le lit**; in bed, **dans le lit**

better, best *adj.*, **meilleur(e)**

beurre *n.m.*, butter

bicyclette *n.f.*, bicycle; **vélo** *n.m.*, bike; bike route **la piste pour cyclistes**

bien *adv.*, fine, well

big *adj.*, **grand(e)**; see Antonyms and Synonyms in the Appendix

billet *n.m.*, ticket

birthday *n.*, **un anniversaire de naissance**

biscotte *n.f.*, Melba toast

black *n.m., adj.*, **noir(e)**

boat *n.*, **un bateau**

boire *v.*, to drink; *past part.* **bu; j'ai bu du lait** I drank some milk

bon, bonne, bons, bonnes *adj.*, good; **les bonbons** *m.*, candies, goodies

book *n.*, **le livre; c'est un livre,** it's a book

boot *n.*, **une botte**; a pair of boots, **une paire de bottes**

boulangerie *n.f.*, bakery

boy *n.*, **le garçon**; little boy, **le petit garçon**

bread *n.*, **le pain**

break *v.*, **casser**; *past part.* **cassé**

breakfast *n.*, **le petit déjeuner**

briefcase *n.*, **une serviette**

brioche *n.f.*, sweet bun

brother *n.*, **un frère**

bruit *n.m.*, noise

bureau *n.m.*, desk, office

bus *n.*, **un bus, un autobus**
but *conj.*, **mais**
butter *n.*, **le beurre**
buy *v.*, **acheter**
by *prep.*, **par**

C

cake *n.*, **le gâteau**
camarade *n.m., f.*, friend
car *n.*, **une voiture, une automobile, une auto;** car accident, **un accident de voiture**
cat *n.*, **le chat, la chatte**
catch *v.*, **attraper**
ce *dem. adj., masc., sing.*, this; **ce médicament** this medicine
celery *n.*, **le céleri**
ces *dem. adj., pl.*, these; **ces pâtisseries** these pastries
c'est, it is; **c'est aujourd'hui . . . ,** today is . . . ; **c'est moi,** it's me (it is I)
cet *dem. adj., masc., sing.* (in front of a masc. sing. noun beginning with silent *h* or a vowel), this; **cet homme** this man; **cet arbre** this tree
cette *dem. adj., fem., sing.*, this; **cette année** this year; **cette jeune fille,** this girl
chair *n.*, **une chaise**
chanson *n.f.*, song
chanter *v.*, to sing; *past part.* **chanté**
chaque *adj.*, each
chat *n.m.*, **chatte** *n.f.*, cat
chauffage *n.m.*, heating system
chaussure *n.f.*, shoe
cheese *n.*, **le fromage**
cheval *n.m.*, horse; **les chevaux,** horses
cheveux *n.m., pl.*, hair
chez moi, at (to) my home (house)
chicken *n.*, **le poulet**
child *n.*, **un (une) enfant;** children, **les enfants** *n.m., f., pl.*
Chine *n.f.*, China
chose *n.f.*, thing
cinéma *n.m.*, movies; **au cinéma,** at (to) the movies (cinema)
circus *n.*, **un cirque**
city *n.*, **la ville**
classe *n.f.*, class; **la classe de français,** French class
close *v.*, **fermer;** *past part.* **fermé; je ferme la fenêtre,** I close the window; **j'ai fermé la porte,** I closed the door

clothes dryer *n.*, **un séchoir**
coat *n.*, **un manteau**
coeur *n.m.*, heart; **par coeur,** by heart (by memory); **apprendre par coeur,** to memorize, learn by heart
coffee *n.*, **le café**
combien *adv.*, how many, how much; **combien de temps?** how much time? (how long?); **depuis combien de temps?** since how long a time?
come *v.*, **venir;** *past part.* **venu; Jacqueline est venue chez moi,** Jacqueline came to my house
commencer *v.*, to begin, to commence; *antonym is* **finir, (se) terminer**
comment *adv.*, how; **Comment ça va?** how are things? (how goes it?); **comment va tout maintenant?** how is everything now? **comment vous appelez-vous?** what is your name?
comprendre *v.*, to understand; *past part.* **compris; j'ai compris,** I understood; see the verb **comprendre** in the Appendix
concert *n.*, **le concert;** at the concert, **au concert**
contraire *n.m., adj.*, opposite, contrary; **au contraire,** on the contrary
corn *n.*, **le maïs**
côté *n.m.*, side; **de l'autre côté,** on the other side
coton *n.m.*, cotton
se coucher *refl. v.*, to go to bed; **je me couche à dix heures,** I go to bed at ten o'clock; see the verb **se coucher** in the Appendix
courir *v.*, to run; **ils courent,** they are running
cousin *n.*, **le cousin, la cousine**
croissant *n.m.*, croissant (bakery item)
cry (weep) *v.*, **pleurer;** *past part.* **pleuré**
cup *n.*, **une tasse;** a cup of coffee, **une tasse de café;** a cup of tea, **une tasse de thé**

D

dance *v.*, **danser;** *past part.* **dansé**
dans *prep.*, in
day *n.*, **le jour**
de *prep.*, of, from; **de bonne heure,** early; **de temps en temps,** from time to time
déjeuner *n.m.*, lunch
demain *adv.*, tomorrow; **demain matin,** tomorrow morning
demeurer *v.*, to reside, to live (in a place); *past part.* **demeuré**
départ *n.m.*, departure

depuis *prep., adv.,* since; **depuis combien de temps?** since how long a time?

dernier, dernière *adj.,* last; **le mois dernier,** last month; **la semaine dernière,** last week; **l'année dernière,** last year

désire *pres. indic., 1st & 3rd pers., sing. of* **désirer,** to desire; *past part.* **désiré**

dessert, *n.,* **le dessert**

devient *pres. indic., 3rd pers., sing. of* **devenir,** to become; *past part.* **devenu; Jacqueline est devenue doctor,** Jacqueline became a doctor

devoir *v.,* to have to, must, should; *past part.* **dû;** *also n.m.,* assignment; see the verb **devoir** in the Appendix

Dieu *n.m.,* God

dîner *n.m.,* dinner; *also v.* to have dinner, to dine; *past part.* **dîné; j'ai dîné à six heures,** I had dinner at 6 o'clock

dining room *n.,* **la salle à manger**

dire *v.,* to say, to tell; *past part.* **dit; j'ai dit la vérité,** I told the truth; see the verb **dire** in the Appendix

dirty *adj.,* **sale**

dix heures, ten o'clock; see Numbers in the Appendix

do *v.,* **faire;** *past part.* **fait; j'ai fait le devoir** I did the assignment; do you have . . . ? **avez-vous . . . ? (as-tu . . . ?)** see the verb **faire** in the Appendix

doctor *n.,* **le docteur, le médecin; une femme docteur,** woman doctor

dog *n.,* **un chien;** a big dog, **un grand chien;** a little dog, **un petit chien**

donner *v.,* to give; *past part.* **donné**

dormir *v.,* to sleep; *past part.* **dormi; j'ai dormi dix heures,** I slept ten hours

dress *n.,* **une robe;** to dress oneself, **s'habiller;** I'm getting dressed, **je m'habille;** he hasn't finished dressing (himself), **il n'a pas fini de s'habiller**

drink *v.,* **boire;** *past part.* **bu;** I drank some milk **j'ai bu du lait**

droite *n.f.,* right (as opposed to *left*); **à droite** to (on) the right

dryer (clothes) *n.,* **un séchoir**

du, of the, from the; some; **du lait** some milk

E

each *adj.,* **chaque**
early *adv.,* **de bonne heure**

eat *v.,* **manger;** *past part.* **mangé;** I am eating, **je mange;** I ate, **j'ai mangé**

école *n.f.,* school; **à l'école,** at school

écouter *v.,* to listen (to); *past part.* **écouté;** I'm listening to the records, **j'écoute les disques;** I listened to the music, **j'ai écouté la musique;** I'm going to listen to the cassette, **je vais écouter la cassette**

écrire *v.,* to write; *past part.* **écrit;** she is writing, **elle écrit;** I am writing a post card, **j'écris une carte postale;** I wrote a letter, **j'ai écrit une lettre**

egg *n.,* **un oeuf**

électricité *n.f.,* electricity

elle *pron. f.,* she, it; her, *as obj. of a prep.,* **avec elle** with her

en *prep.,* in; **en hiver** in winter; **en général** in general, generally; **en retard** late

end *v.* **finir, (se) terminer**

enfant *n.m., f.,* child

enjoy oneself *refl. v.,* **s'amuser;** I am enjoying myself, **je m'amuse**

entendre *v.,* to hear; *past part.* **entendu; j'entends les oiseaux,** I hear the birds; **j'ai entendu le bruit,** I heard the noise

envoyez-moi, send me

est *pres. indic., 3rd pers., sing. of* **être** to be; **est-ce . . .?** is it . . .? **est-ce que . . .?** is it that . . .? (These words are usually placed at the beginning of an interrogative statement); **Est-ce que vous vous lavez tous les matins?** Do you wash yourself every morning? See the verb **être** in the Appendix

et *conj.,* and

était *imperfect indic. of* **être,** to be; see the verb **être** and the review of basic French idioms with **être** in the Appendix

été *past part. of* **être** to be; also *n.m.,* summer; **il fait chaud en été,** it is warm in summer

être *v.,* to be; *past part.* **été;** see the verb **être** in the Appendix

étudier *v.,* to study; see the verb **étudier** in the Appendix

éveiller *v.,* to wake up

evening *n.,* **le soir;** every evening, **tous les soirs**

every morning, **tous les matins;** every day, **tous les jours;** every night, **toutes les nuits;** every evening, **tous les soirs**

expensive *adj.,* **cher, chère; ce livre est cher,** this book is expensive; **cette maison est chère,** this house is expensive

extraordinaire *adj.,* extraordinary

F

F (Franc) *n.m.,* franc (For the current international exchange rate of French francs, consult a commercial bank or a travel bureau.)

facile *adj.,* easy; **facile à porter,** easy-to-wear; **prêt à porter,** ready-to-wear

faible *adj.,* weak; see Antonyms and Synonyms in the Appendix

faire *v.,* to do, to make; see the verb **faire** in the Appendix

fall (autumn) *n.,* **l'automne** *m.;* see the seasons of the year in the Appendix

falloir *v.,* to be necessary; *past part.* **fallu**

fast (rapid) *adj.,* **rapide**

fat *adj.,* **gros, grosse**

father *n.,* **le père, le papa**

faucet, *n.,* **le robinet**

faut *pres. indic., 3rd pers., sing.* of **falloir,** to be necessary; **il faut,** it is necessary

feel better (health), **aller mieux;** I'm feeling better, **je vais mieux;** see the review of basic French idioms with **aller** in the Appendix

femme *n.f.,* woman

fermer *v.,* to close; *past part.* **fermé; j'ai fermé la fenêtre,** I closed the window

finir *v.,* to finish, to end, to terminate; *past part.* **fini; j'ai fini le devoir,** I finished the assignment

first *adj.,* **premier, première**

fleur *n.f.,* flower; **le marché aux fleurs,** flower market

for *prep.,* **pour**

forger *v.,* to forge (iron); **en forgeant,** by forging; **forgeron** *n.m.,* blacksmith, ironsmith

forget *v.,* **oublier;** *past part.* **oublié; j'ai oublié,** I forgot

fort, forte *adj.,* strong; see Antonyms and Synonyms in the Appendix

fraise *n.f.,* strawberry

French (language) *m.,* **le français;** I like French, **j'aime le français;** French class, **la classe de français**

frère *n.m.,* brother

friend *n.,* **un ami, une amie;** friendship, **l'amitié** *n.f.;* friendly, **amical(e), amicalement** (closing of a friendly letter)

from *prep.,* **de;** from time to time, **de temps en temps**

fruit *n.,* **le fruit**

fuir *v.,* to flee; *past part.* **fui**

funny *adj.,* **drôle**

G

garçon *n.m.,* boy; **le petit garçon,** the little boy; **le grand garçon,** the big boy

garden *n.,* **le jardin**

gare *n.f.,* station (railroad, bus, *etc.*)

gauche *adj., n.m.,* left; **à gauche,** to (on) the left

generally, **en général**

get up *refl. v.,* **se lever; je me lève à six heures,** I get up at six o'clock; see the verb **se lever** in the Appendix

girl *n.,* **la jeune fille**

go *v.,* **aller**

go to bed *refl. v.,* **se coucher; je me couche à dix heures,** I go to bed at ten o'clock; see the verb **se coucher** in the Appendix

God *n.,* **Dieu**

good *adj.,* **bon, bons, bonne, bonnes; un bon garçon,** a good boy; **une bonne jeune fille,** a good girl; **de bons amis,** good friends; **de bonnes personnes,** good persons

good-bye, **au revoir**

grand, grande *adj.,* big, large, tall; **un grand garçon,** a big boy; **une grande jeune fille,** a big girl

H

h., *abbreviation for* **heure** hour

habit *n.m.,* clothes, robe (of a monk or nun)

hair *n.,* **les cheveux** *m.*

ham *n.,* **le jambon**

hand *n.,* **la main**

handsome *adj.,* **beau, bel; un beau monsieur,** a handsome gentleman; **un bel homme,** a handsome man

happy *adj.* **heureux, heureuse; content, contente;** see Antonyms and Synonyms in the Appendix

haricots verts *n.m.,* string beans

have *v.,* **avoir;** *past part.* **eu;** to have a good time, **s'amuser;** I'm having a good time here, **je m'amuse ici;** I had a good lunch, **j'ai eu un bon déjeuner;** see the verb **avoir** and the review of basic French idioms with **avoir** in the Appendix

he *pron.,* **il**

hear *v.,* **entendre;** *past part.* **entendu; j'ai entendu un bruit,** I heard a noise

heart *n.,* **le coeur**

heating system *n.*, **le chauffage**

here *adv.*, **ici**

heure *n.f.*, hour; **à cette heure,** at this moment, at this hour, now

hier *adv.*, yesterday

hiver *n.m.*, winter; see the seasons of the year in the Appendix

hold *v.*, **tenir;** *past part.* **tenu**

home, **à la maison;** at my home, **à ma maison** *or* **chez moi**

homme *n.m.*, man

horizontalement *adv.*, horizontally

horses *n.*, **les chevaux** *m.*

hour *n.*, **l'heure** *f.*

house *n.*, **la maison**

how *adv.*, **comment;** how are things? **comment ça va?** how are you? **comment allez-vous?** *or* **comment vas-tu?** how many, how much *adv.*, **combien;** how old are you? **quel âge avez-vous?** *or* **quel âge as-tu?**

hungry, to be *v.*, **avoir faim;** I am hungry, **j'ai faim;** see the verb **avoir** and the review of basic French idioms with **avoir** in the Appendix

hurry *v.*, **se dépêcher;** I'm hurrying, **je me dépêche**

husband *n.*, **le mari, l'époux** *m.*

I

ici *adv.*, here

il *pron.*, *m.s.*, he; *pl.*, **ils,** they

il y a, there is . . . ; there are . . .

in *prep.*, **dans;** in order to, **pour;** in school, **à l'école;** in town, **en ville**

intelligent *adj.*, **intelligent(e)**

invitation *n.*, **invitation** *f.*

is it . . . ? **est-ce . . . ?**

is there . . . ? **y a-t-il . . . ?**

it is . . . , **c'est;** it's me, **c'est moi;** it is one o'clock, **il est une heure;** it is two thirty, **il est deux heures et demie;** see Numbers in the Appendix

---

J

jamais *adv.*, never

jardin *n.m.*, garden

jeune fille *n.f.*, girl

---

jouer *v.*, to play; *past part.* **joué; jouer à la balle,** to play ball

jour *n.m.*, day

jupe *n.f.*, skirt

K

king *n.*, **le roi**

kitchen *n.*, **la cuisine**

know (how) *v.*, **savoir;** *past part.* **su; je sais jouer du piano,** I know how to play the piano

know (to be acquainted with a person, place) *v.*, **connaître;** *past part.* **connu; je connais Jacqueline,** I know Jacqueline; **je connais Paris,** I know Paris

---

L

l' *def. art.*, *m., f.*, the (in front of a noun beginning with a vowel or silent *h*); **l'arbre,** the tree; **l'hôtel,** the hotel

la *def. art.*, *f.*, the; **la maison,** the house

lait *n.m.*, milk; **du lait,** some milk

laitue *n.f.*, lettuce

lamp *n.*, **la lampe**

large *adj.*, **grand(e)**

late *adv.*, **tard;** later, **plus tard;** to be late for work, **être en retard pour le travail**

se laver *refl. v.*, to wash oneself; see the verb **se laver** in the Appendix

le *def. art.*, *m.*, the; **le livre,** the book

learn *v.*, **apprendre;** *past part.* **appris; j'ai appris la leçon,** I learned the lesson

lécher *v.*, to lick; **faire du lèche-vitrines,** to go window shopping

leçon *n.f.*, lesson

left (as opposed to *right*), **gauche; à gauche,** to (on, at) the left

les *def. art.*, *m.f.*, *pl.*, the; **les billets,** the tickets

letter *n.*, **la lettre**

lettuce *n.*, **la laitue**

se lever *refl. v.*, to get up; **je me lève à six heures,** I get up at six o'clock; see the verb **se lever** in the Appendix

lieu *n.m.*, place; **avoir lieu,** to take place; see the verb **avoir** and the review of basic French idioms with **avoir** in the Appendix

like *v.*, **aimer bien;** I like writing in French, **j'aime bien écrire en français**

lire v., to read; *past part.* **lu;** see the verb **lire** in the Appendix

live (in a place) v., **demeurer;** *past part.* **demeuré; je demeure dans une jolie petite maison,** I live in a small pretty house

livre n.m., book; n.f., pound; **une livre de beurre,** a pound of butter

love v., **aimer;** I love you, **je vous aime (je t'aime)**

lu *past part.* of **lire,** to read; **j'ai lu deux livres la semaine dernière,** I read two books last week; see the verb **lire** in the Appendix

lunch n., **le déjeuner;** breakfast, **le petit déjeuner**

M

ma *poss. adj., f.,* my; **ma mère,** my mother; **ma maison,** my house

magasin n.m., store; **un grand magasin,** department store; **aux grands magasins,** to (at) the department stores

mai n.m., May; see the Appendix for seasons of the year

main n.f., hand

maintenant *adv.,* now

mais *conj.,* but

maison n.f., house

make v., **faire;** see the verb **faire** in the Appendix

malade *adj.,* sick, ill; **être malade,** to be sick; see the verb **être** in the Appendix

man n., **un homme**

manche n.f., sleeve

manger v., to eat; *past part.* **mangé; j'ai mangé,** I ate (I did eat, I have eaten)

marcher v., to walk; to take a walk, **faire une promenade;** see the verb **faire** and the review of basic French idioms with **faire** in the Appendix

mashed potatoes n., **la purée de pommes de terre;** potato, **la pomme de terre**

matin n.m., morning; **tous les matins,** every morning

me *pron.,* myself, (to) me; **je me lave,** I wash myself; **elle me parle,** she is talking to me; **avec moi,** with me; see the verb **se laver** in the Appendix

meal n., **le repas**

meilleur(e) *adj.,* better, best

mentionner v., to mention; **mentionnez trois choses,** mention three things

merci, thank you; **merci mille fois,** thank you very much

mère n.f., mother

mes *poss. adj., pl.,* my; **mes amis,** my friends

mettre v., to put, to place; *past part.* **mis; je mets la valise sur le lit,** I'm putting the suitcase on the bed; **j'ai mis les fleurs dans un vase il y a une heure,** I put the flowers in a vase an hour ago; see the verb **mettre** in the Appendix

mieux *adv.,* better

milk n., **le lait;** some milk, **du lait**

Mlle (abbreviation for **Mademoiselle,** Miss)

modern *adj.,* **moderne,** *m. & f.*

moi *pron.,* me *(when obj. of a prep.);* **avec moi** with me

moine n.m., monk

mois n.m., month; see the months of the year in the Appendix

moment n.m., moment; **à ce moment,** at this moment, now

monkey n., **le singe**

monsieur n.m., gentleman, sir, mister; (abbreviation in French is **M.**)

monster n., **le monstre**

monter v., to climb, to mount, to get on (in) a bus, car, *etc.*

month n., **le mois;** see the months of the year in the Appendix

morning n., **le matin;** every morning, **tous les matins**

mother n., **la mère**

mourir v., to die; *past part.* **mort(e); Monsieur Durant est mort hier,** Mr. Durant died yesterday; **Madame Dupont est morte,** Mrs. Dupont has died

my *poss. adj.,* **mon, ma, mes; mon ami(e), ma maison, mes ami(e)s**

my name is . . ., **mon nom est . . .; je m'appelle . . .; je suis . . .**

N

naître v., to be born; *past part.* **né; je suis né(e), le premier avril,** I was born on April 1st; **Monique est née le quinze mai,** Monique was born on May 15th; **Pierre est né le vingt juin,** Peter was born on June 20th

napkin n., **la serviette de table**

ne *adv.* This word is placed in front of a verb with **pas** after the verb to make the verb negative; **je ne sais pas,** I don't know; **je n'ai pas d'argent,** I haven't any money

necessary, to be *v.,* **falloir;** *past part.* **fallu;** it is necessary, **il faut (il est nécessaire); il a fallu partir tout de suite,** it was necessary to leave right away

neige *n.f.,* snow; **j'aime marcher dans la neige,** I like to walk in the snow

neiger *v.,* to snow; **il neige,** it's snowing

n'est-ce pas? isn't it so?

never *adv.,* **jamais**

new *adj.,* **nouveau, nouvel, nouvelle, nouveaux, nouvelles; un nouveau manteau,** a new overcoat; **un nouvel ami,** a new friend *(male);* **une nouvelle amie,** a new friend *(female);* **de nouveaux jouets,** new toys; **de nouvelles voitures,** new automobiles

next Saturday afternoon, samedi prochain de l'après-midi

night *n.,* **la nuit**

no one *pron.,* **personne;** I see no one, **je ne vois personne**

nobody *pron.,* **personne;** nobody is here, **personne n'est ici;** *n.f.,* a person; **une personne est dans l'autobus,** one person is in the bus

nom *n.m.,* name; **quel est votre nom?** what is your name? **mon nom est . . .,** my name is . . .

nommer *v.,* to name; *past part.* **nommé; nommez deux choses . . .,** name two things . . .

non *adv.,* no

nothing *pron.,* **rien;** I see nothing (I don't see anything) **je ne vois rien**

now *adv.,* **maintenant**

nuit *n.f.,* night

number *n.,* **le numéro**

O

oeufs *n.m., pl.,* eggs

of *prep.,* **de**

office *n.,* **le bureau;** to (at) the office, **au bureau**

okay, d'accord, okay

on *pron.,* one, someone, anyone; **on est à la porte,** someone is at the door; **on ne sait jamais,** one never knows

on time *adv.,* **à l'heure**

one o'clock, une heure; it is one o'clock, **il est une heure**

open *v.,* **ouvrir;** *past part.* **ouvert;** I'm opening the window, **j'ouvre la fenêtre;** I opened the door, **j'ai ouvert la porte**

or *conj.,* **ou**

où *adv.,* where; **où est-ce que vous vous habillez?** where do you get dressed?

oui *adv.,* yes

ouvrir *v.,* to open

oversleep *v.,* **dépasser l'heure du réveil;** I overslept, **j'ai dépassé l'heure du réveil**

P

page *n.,* **la page**

pain *n.m.,* bread

pan *n.,* **une casserole**

papeterie *n.f.,* stationery shop

par *prep.,* by

parc *n.m.,* park

parler *v.,* to talk, to speak; **parlez-vous français?** do you speak French? *past part.* **parlé; j'ai parlé avec mes amis,** I spoke with my friends; see the verb **parler** in the Appendix

participer *v.,* to participate

partir *v.,* to leave; *past. part.* **parti; Robert est parti à une heure et Debbie est partie à deux heures,** Robert left at one o'clock and Debbie left at two o'clock

passer *v.,* to spend (time), to pass by, to go by

path *n.,* **une piste**

pâtisserie *n.f.,* pastry, pastry shop

pay *v.,* **payer**

peas *n.,* **les petits pois,** *m.*

penser *v.,* to think; *past part.* **pensé**

père *n.m.,* father

petit(e) *adj.,* little, small; **le petit garçon,** the little boy; **la petite maison,** the small house

petit déjeuner *n.m.,* breakfast

peur *n.f.,* fear

piano *n.,* **le piano**

plane (airplane) *n.,* **un avion;** in the plane, **dans l'avion;** by air mail, **par avion**

play *v.,* **jouer;** *past part.* **joué;** to play tennis, **jouer au tennis;** to play ball, **jouer à la balle;** to play the piano, **jouer du piano**

pleasant *adj.,* **agréable**

please, s'il vous plaît *or* **s'il te plaît**

pleuvoir *v.,* to rain

plomberie *n.f.,* plumbing

policeman *n.,* **un agent de police**

pommes de terre *n.f.,* potatoes; **la purée de pommes de terre,** mashed potatoes pot *n.*, **une marmite;** pots and pans, **une batterie de cuisine**

pour *prep.*, for, in order to; **ce cadeau est pour vous,** this gift is for you; **il faut manger pour vivre,** it is necessary to eat in order to live

pourquoi *adv.*, why

pouvoir *v.*, to be able, can; *past part.* **pu**

préférer *v.*, to prefer; **je préfère,** I prefer

premier, première *adj.*, first; **le premier homme,** the first man; **la première femme,** the first woman

prendre *v.*, to take, to have (something to eat or drink); *past part.* **pris; je vais prendre le train,** I'm going to take the train; **je vais prendre une pâtisserie,** I'm going to have a pastry; see the verb **prendre** in the Appendix

pretty *adj.*, **joli, jolie; un joli arbre,** à pretty tree; **une jolie plante,** a pretty plant

price *n.*, **le prix;** what is the price? **quel est le prix?**

printemps *n.m.*, spring (season of the year); see the seasons of the year in the Appendix

pris *past part. of* **prendre,** to take

prix *n.m.*, price, prize; **le grand prix,** the grand (first) prize

profession *n.f.*, profession

proverbe *n.m.*, proverb (There is a French proverb with English equivalent at the end of each Review Test.)

purchase *v.*, **acheter;** a purchase, **un achat**

Q

qualité *n.f.*, quality; **c'est de bonne qualité?** it's good quality?

quand *conj.*, when; synonym is **lorsque**

que *pron.*, what; also *conj.*, that; **que désirez-vous?** what do you want? (what do you desire?); **je sais que vous êtes intelligent(e),** I know that you are intelligent

quel, quelle, quels, quelles *adj.*, what, which; **quel âge avez-vous?** how old are you? **quel jour est-ce aujourd'hui?** what day is it today? **quel temps fait-il en été?** what's the weather like in summer? **quelle adresse?** what (which) address? **quels garçons?** what (which) boys? **quelles jeunes filles?** what (which) girls?

quelque chose *pron.*, something

quelqu'un *pron.*, someone, somebody

qu'est-ce que *pron.*, what *(as a dir. obj.)*; **qu'est-ce que vous dites?** what are you saying?

qu'est-ce que c'est? what is it?

qu'est-ce qu'il (elle) fait? what is he (she) doing?

question *n.*, **la question**

qui *pron.*, who, whom, which; **qui êtes-vous?** who are you? **qui cherchez-vous?** whom are you looking for? **avec qui allez-vous au cinéma?** with whom are you going to the movies? **cette chose qui est ici est pour qui?** this thing which is here is for whom?

qui est-ce? who is it?

quick *adj.*, quickly; *adv.*, **vite**

quinze, fifteen; see Numbers in the Appendix

quoi *pron.*, what *(as obj. of a prep.);* **avec quoi?** with what?

R

radiator *n.*, **le radiateur**

rain *v.*, **pleuvoir;** *past part.* **plu; il pleut,** it's raining; **il a plu,** it rained

read *v.*, **lire;** *past part.* **lu; je peux lire,** I can read; **je lis,** I read; **j'ai lu un livre hier,** I read a book yesterday; see the verb **lire** in the Appendix

receive *v.*, **recevoir;** *past part.* **reçu; merci pour le basket-ball que j'ai reçu,** thank you for the basketball that I received

red *adj.*, **rouge; une jupe rouge,** a red skirt; **un vélo rouge,** a red bike

refuse *v.*, **refuser;** *past part.* **refusé**

remain *v.*, **rester;** *past part.* **resté; Robert est resté à la maison,** Robert remained (stayed) home; **Janine est restée seule,** Janine remained alone

repas *n.m.*, meal

reply *v.*, **répondre;** *past part.* **répondu;** I'm answering the letter, **je réponds à la lettre;** I answered the post card, **j'ai répondu à la carte postale; répondez, s'il vous plaît,** answer, please; **répondez-vous?** are you answering? *or* do you answer?

réponse *n.f.*, reply, answer, response

reside *v.*, **demeurer;** *past part.* **demeuré;** I reside (live) in this house, **je demeure dans cette maison;** I lived (resided) here last year, **j'ai demeuré ici l'année dernière (passée)**

respond *v.*, **répondre;** *past part.* **répondu**

ressembler *v.*, to resemble, to look like

rester *v.*, to remain, to stay; *past part.* **resté**

réunion *n.f.*, reunion, meeting

rien *n.*, *pron.*, nothing; **je n'ai rien,** I have nothing; **rien n'est ici,** nothing is here; **ce n'est rien,** it's nothing

right (as opposed to *left*), **droite; à droite,** to (on, at) the right; to be right, **avoir raison;** I am right, **j'ai raison;** see the verb **avoir** and the review of basic French idioms with **avoir** in the Appendix

rire *v.*, to laugh; *past part.* **ri**

roll (bread) *n.*, **un petit pain**

romantique *adj.*, romantic

rue *n.f.* street

run *v.* **courir; ils courent,** they are running

S

sad *adj.*, **triste**

sale *adj.*, dirty, soiled

salt *n.*, **le sel**

samedi *n.m.*, Saturday; see the days of the week in the Appendix

sand *n.*, **le sable**

savoir *v.*, to know (how); *past part.* **su; savez-vous . . .?** do you know (how) . . .? **savez-vous jouer du piano?** do you know how to play the piano? **savez-vous la réponse?** do you know the answer? **j'ai su la réponse,** I knew the answer; see the verb **savoir** in the Appendix

say *v.*, **dire;** *past part.* **dit;** see the verb **dire** in the Appendix

school *n.*, **l'école** *f.;* see the Appendix for review of basic vocabulary by topics

se *refl. pron.*, *3rd pers.*, *sing.*, *pl.*, himself, herself, oneself, itself, themselves; see for example the verb **se laver** in the Appendix

seashore *n.*, **le bord de la mer;** the beach, **la plage**

see *v.*, **voir;** *past part.* **vu; je vois mon ami,** I see my friend; I saw a French movie, **j'ai vu un film français**

semaine *n.f.*, week; see the days of the week in the Appendix

she *pron.*, **elle;** she is writing a letter, **elle écrit une lettre**

shirt *n.*, **la chemise**

shop window *n.*, **la vitrine;** to go shopping, **faire des emplettes;** to go window shopping, **faire du lèche-vitrines;** shopping bag, **le sac (le filet) à provisions;** shopping cart, **le chariot**

short *adj.*, **petit(e)**

si *conj.*, if; *adv.*, so; **si vous voulez apprendre, étudiez la leçon,** If you want to learn, study the lesson; **Pauline est si belle,** Pauline is so beautiful

sick *adj.*, **malade;** to be sick, **être malade**

sidewalk *n.*, **le trottoir**

s'il vous plaît, please

sing *v.*, **chanter;** *past part.* **chanté**

sister *n.*, **la soeur**

sleep *v.*, **dormir;** *past part.* **dormi;** I sleep, **je dors;** I slept, **j'ai dormi**

soiled *adj.*, **sale**

soir *n.m.*, evening; **tous les soirs,** every evening; **ce soir,** this evening, tonight

some milk, **du lait**

somebody (someone) *pron.*, **quelqu'un**

something *pron.*, **quelque chose**

son *poss. adj.*, *m.*, his, her; **son père, son (ami, amie);** *also n.m.*, sound

speak *v.*, **parler;** *past part.* **parlé;** see the verb **parler** in the Appendix

spring (season) *n.*, **le printemps;** see the seasons of the year in the Appendix

stage *n.*, **la scène;** on stage, **sur la scène**

station *n.*, **la gare**

stay *v.*, **rester;** *past part.* **resté; Monsieur Durand est resté dans la cuisine et sa femme est restée dans le salon,** Mr. Durand stayed in the kitchen and his wife stayed in the living room

store *n.*, **le magasin;** department store, **le grand magasin;** store window, **la vitrine**

strawberry *n.*, **la fraise**

street *n.*, **la rue**

string beans *n. pl.*, **les haricots verts,** *m.*

strong *adj.*, **fort(e); le garçon est fort et la jeune fille est forte, aussi,** the boy is strong and the girl is strong, too; see Antonyms and Synonyms in the Appendix

stupid *adj.*, **stupide, bête**

sucre *n.m.*, sugar

suit *n.*, **un costume**

summer *n.*, **l'été,** *m.;* see the seasons of the year in the Appendix

summer clothes *n.*, **les vêtements d'été**

sun *n.*, **le soleil;** to take a sun bath, **prendre un bain de soleil;** see the verb **prendre** in the Appendix

sur *prep.*, on

surprised *adj.*, **surpris(e)**

sweater *n.*, **le pull, le pullover, le chandail**

swim *v.* **nager;** *past part.* **nagé;** I swim **je nage;** I swam **j'ai nagé;** swim suit **le maillot de bain**

T

tablecloth *n.*, **la nappe**

se taire *refl. v.*, to be quiet, silent; *past part.* **tu;** see the verb **se taire** in the Appendix

take *v.*, **prendre;** *past part.* **pris;** see the verb **prendre** in the Appendix

take place *v.*, **avoir lieu;** see the verb **avoir** and the review of basic French idioms with **avoir** in the Appendix

talk *v.*, **parler;** *past part.* **parlé;** see the verb **parler** in the Appendix

tall *adj.*, **grand(e);** see Antonyms and Synonyms in the Appendix

téléphone *n.m.*, telephone

télévision *n.f.*, television; **la télé,** TV

tell *v.*, **dire;** *past part.* **dit;** see the verb **dire** in the Appendix

temps *n.m.*, weather; **quel temps fait-il?** what's the weather like? **il fait beau,** the weather is beautiful; see the verb **faire** and the review of basic French idioms with **faire** in the Appendix; the word **le temps** also means time (in general, a period of time); **Je n'ai pas le temps d'aller au cinéma ce soir,** I don't have the time to go to the movies tonight

tenir *v.*, to hold; *past part.* **tenu**

thank you, **merci;** thank you very much, **merci mille fois; merci bien; merci beaucoup**

theater *n.*, **le théâtre;** at the theater, **au théâtre**

there are . . ., **il y a . . .;** there are many people in this plane, **il y a beaucoup de personnes dans cet avion**

there is . . ., **il y a . . .;** there is a fly in my soup, **il y a une mouche dans ma soupe**

thing *n.*, **la chose**

ticket *n.*, **le billet**

to *prep.*, **à;** to the movies, **au cinéma;** to the house, **à la maison;** to the boy, **au garçon;** to the girl, **à la jeune fille;** to the children, **aux enfants**

today is . . ., **c'est aujourd'hui . . .**

toi *pron.*, you (when obj. of a prep.); **avec toi** with you; **pour toi,** for you

tomato *n.*, **la tomate**

tomorrow *adv.*, **demain**

toujours *adv.*, always

Tour de France *n.m.*, National Bicycle Race (around France)

tous *adj., m., pl.*, all, every; **tous les matins,** every morning; **tous les soirs,** every evening; **tous les jours,** every day

tout *pron.*, all; **tout est bien qui finit bien,** all is well that ends well

towel *n.*, **la serviette de toilette**

train *n.*, **le train**

travailler *v.*, to work; *past part.* **travaillé; je travaille tous les jours,** I work every day; **j'ai travaillé hier,** I worked yesterday

travel *v.*, **voyager;** *past part.* **voyagé**

très *adv.*, very; **très bien,** very well

triste *adj.*, sad

trois, three; see Numbers in the Appendix

trousers *n.*, **le pantalon**

trouver *v.*, to find; **se trouver** *refl. v.*, to be located; *past part.* **trouvé**

tu *pron.*, you (2nd pers., sing., familiar form); **tu veux aller au cinéma avec moi?** do you want to go to the movies with me?

tuer *v.*, to kill; *past part.* **tué; un grand camion a tué le pauvre petit animal,** a big truck killed the poor little animal

two thirty (o'clock), **deux heures et demie;** it is two thirty, **il est deux heures et demie;** I'm going home at two thirty, **je vais chez moi à deux heures et demie;** see Numbers in the Appendix

U

user *v.*, to wear out; *past part.* **usé; ces gants sont usés,** these gloves are worn out; **ces chaussures sont usées,** these shoes are worn out

utilisable *adj.*, useful

V

va *pres. indic., 3rd pers., sing.* of **aller,** to go; **Joseph va à l'école,** Joseph is going to school; see the verb **aller** and the review of basic French idioms with **aller** in the Appendix

valoir *v.*, to be worth; *past part.* **valu**

vase *n.*, **le vase**

vendre *v.*, to sell; *past part.* **vendu; un vendeur,** salesman; **une vendeuse,** saleswoman

verticalement *adj.*, vertically

veux-tu? do you want? see the verb **vouloir** in the Appendix

ville *n.f.*, city

vingt, twenty; see Numbers in the Appendix

violin, *n.*, **le violon**

vite *adj.*, quick; *adv.*, quickly

vitrine *n.f.,* store window

vivre *v.,* to live; *past part.* **vécu**

voir *v.,* to see; *past part.* **vu**

vos *pl. of* **votre,** your; **vos chaussures** your shoes; **vos ami(e)s** your friends

votre *poss. adj., sing.,* your; **votre ami(e),** your friend

voudrais *1st & 2nd pers., sing., cond. of* **vouloir,** to want; see the verb **vouloir** in the Appendix

voulez-vous? do you want?

vouloir *v.,* to want; *past part.* **voulu;** see the verb **vouloir** in the Appendix

vous *pron.,* you *(pl., sing., polite);* also *refl. pron.,* yourself, yourselves; **voulez-vous venir chez moi?** do you want to come to my house? **à quelle heure est-ce que vous vous couchez?** at what time do you go to bed? **je vous donne un livre,** I give you a book

voyager *v.,* to travel; *past part.* **voyagé; je voyage tous les étés,** I travel every summer; **l'été passé j'ai voyagé en France,** last summer I traveled in France

W

walk *v.,* **marcher;** *past part.* **marché;** to take a walk, **faire une promenade;** see the verb **faire** and review of basic French idioms with **faire** in the Appendix

want *v.,* **vouloir;** see the verb **vouloir** in the Appendix

watch television, regarder la télé (la télévision)

water-ski *v.,* **faire du ski nautique**

weak *adj.,* **faible;** see Antonyms and Synonyms in the Appendix

week *n.,* **la semaine;** see days of the week in review of basic vocabulary by topics in the Appendix

well *adv.,* **bien**

what do you want? que voulez-vous? (que veux-tu?); see the verb **vouloir** in the Appendix; see also **que** in this list

what is it? **qu'est-ce que c'est?**

what is the address? **quelle est l'adresse?**

what is the date? **quelle est la date?**

what is your name? **comment vous appelez-vous? quel est votre nom?**

what time is it? **quelle heure est-il?**

what's the weather like in summer? **quel temps fait-il en été** see the verb **faire** and review of basic French idioms with **faire** in the Appendix

when *conj.,* **quand, lorsque**

where *adv.,* **où**

which cinéma? **quel cinéma?** see **quel** in this list

who, whom *pron.,* **qui;** see **qui** in this list

who is it? **qui est-ce**

why *adv.,* **pourquoi**

wife *n.,* **la femme, l'épouse** *n.f.*

window *n.,* **la fenêtre;** to go window shopping, **faire du lèche-vitrines**

windsurfing, to go *v.,* **faire de la planche à voile**

wine *n.,* **le vin**

winter *n.,* **l'hiver** *m.;* see the seasons of the year in the review of basic vocabulary by topics in the Appendix

with *prep.,* **avec**

woman *n.,* **la femme**

write *v.,* **écrire;** *past part.* **écrit;** she is writing a letter, **elle écrit une lettre;** she wrote a letter, **elle a écrit une lettre**

wrong, to be *v.,* **avoir tort;** see the verb **avoir** and the review of basic French idioms with **avoir** in the Appendix

Y

y a-t-il . . .? is there . . .? are there . . .?

y avait-il . . .? was there . . .? were there . . .?

year *n.,* **un an; une année**

yes *adv.,* **oui**

yesterday *adv.,* **hier**

you *pron.,* **tu** *(2nd pers., sing., familiar form);* **vous** *(pl. and sing., polite form)*

Index of idioms, verbal expressions, proverbs and key words showing their location in this book

◆

The location number given is the *Devoir* number. The abbreviation RT plus a number is the Review Test number. A reflexive verb is listed under the verb, not under the reflexive pronoun.

Answers

NOTE TO USERS OF THIS BOOK. In the 40 Devoirs, Exercise I contains words, phrases, and idiomatic expressions related in thought in French with English equivalents. The model sentences in Exercise I illustrate their use. Students are requested to write their own sentences, imitating the models in French. Therefore, what students will write in French will vary greatly. For that reason, there are no sample sentences given here for Exercise I in the 40 Devoirs. The model sentences in French may be used to copy on the lines for practice if students are not yet able to write simple sentences of their own. Then they can compare what they wrote in French with the model sentences.

DEVOIR 1

II. 1. appelle 2. ai 3. lève 4. matins 5. donne **III.** 1. Je m'appelle (plus your name). 2. J'ai (number) ans. 3. Je me lève à six heures et demie. **IV.** Je m'appelle (plus your name). J'ai (number) ans. Tous les matins je prends un bon petit déjeuner. **V.** Il boit du lait. **VI.** se lever **VII.** fraise **VIII.** 1. du lait 2. des oeufs 3. une brioche **IX.** 1. ma 2. mai 3. mais 4. mois 5. on 6. son **X.** 1. Je me lève 2. Je prends

DEVOIR 2

II. 1. fait 2. froid 3. printemps 4. en 5. aujourd'hui **III.** 1. Il fait chaud en été. 2. Il fait froid en hiver. 3. Il fait beau au printemps. 4. Il fait frais en automne. 5. Il fait doux aujourd'hui. Je vais au parc. **IV.** Il fait frais en automne. Il fait froid en hiver. Il fait beau au printemps. Il fait chaud en été. Il fait doux aujourd'hui. Je vais au parc. **V.** Il lit un livre. **VI.** lait **VII.** lit **VIII.** 1. fait 2. chaud 3. froid **IX.** 1. ai 2. la 3. lit **X.** doux (beau, frais, chaud)

DEVOIR 3

II. 1. il 2. neige 3. me 4. moi 5. air **III.** 1. Quand il pleut, je reste à la maison. 2. Quand il neige, je vais au parc. 3. J'aime me promener dans un parc. 4. Les quatre saisons de l'année sont le printemps, l'été, l'automne, l'hiver. 5. Il neige en hiver. **IV.** Je reste à la maison quand il pleut. Je vais au parc quand il neige. J'aime me promener dans le parc quand il neige. J'aime lire chez moi quand il pleut. J'aime être en plein air quand il fait beau. **V.** Elle danse. **VI.** faire **VII.** mois **VIII.** 1. Je danse. 2. Je lis. **IX.** Le garçon boit du lait. **X.** me, neige

REVIEW TEST 1

I. Je m'appelle (plus your name). J'ai (number) ans. Je me lève à six heures et demie. Tous les matins je prends un bon petit déjeuner. **II.** Il fait chaud en été. Il fait froid en hiver. Il fait beau au printemps. Il fait frais en automne. **III.** J'aime lire chez moi quand il pleut. Je vais au parc quand il neige. Je vais au parc quand il fait doux (beau). J'aime me promener dans un parc. **IV.** 1. lève 2. matins, bon 3. froid, chaud 4. fait **V.** 1. du lait 2. des oeufs 3. des brioches **VI.** 1. Il lit un livre. 2. Elle danse. 3. Il boit du lait. **VII.** se lever **VIII.** fraise **IX.** dans **X.** 1. an 2. dans 3. de

DEVOIR 4

II. 1. vous 2. mal 3. vais 4. la 5. passer **III.** 1. Je vais bien (mal). 2. Mon ami(e) va bien (mal). 3. Je reste à la maison quand je suis malade. 4. Cette année je vais passer deux semaines à la campagne. 5. Aujourd'hui je vais au parc. **IV.** 1. je 2. vais 3. toujours 4. bien 5. mal 6. mieux **V.** Ils courent. **VI.** 1. bien 2. mal 3. mieux **VII.** Cet été je vais passer une semaine à la campagne. **VIII.** Je vais passer deux semaines à la campagne. **IX.** 1. une balle 2. un ballon 3. une bicyclette **X.** Cher ami Robert (Chère amie Janine), Je vais passer une semaine à la campagne. Je pars demain. Amicalement, (plus your name). **XI.** bien, mal, seize (or whatever your age is), tous

DEVOIR 5

II. 1. ai 2. faim 3. soif 4. ai 5. autre **III.** ai, ai, mange, bois, l'habitude, moi, manger, restaurant **IV.** 1. Ce n'est pas un chapeau. C'est un gâteau. 2. Oui, il est délicieux. **V.** 1. du lait 2. des biscottes 3. du beurre 4. des fraises 5. du céleri 6. des croissants **VI.** 1. Je mange quand j'ai faim. 2. Je bois quand j'ai soif. 3. J'ai l'habitude de manger chez moi. **VII.** Merci mille fois pour l'invitation. Je vais dîner chez moi. Je vais toujours mal.

DEVOIR 6

II. 1. il 2. y 3. de 4. au 5. à **III.** y, près, a, joue, vais, jouer **IV.** 1. Il y a deux parcs dans ma ville. 2. Dans un parc on trouve des arbres (trees), des bancs (benches), et des fleurs. 3. Je joue à la balle dans un parc. 4. Je joue au tennis dans un parc. 5. Je vais au parc pour jouer à la balle. **V.** Elle est dans un parc. Elle joue à la balle. **VI.** Je vais au parc pour jouer au tennis. **VII.** vais, jouer, au tennis

REVIEW TEST 2

I. Je vais mal aujourd'hui. Je vais à la campagne. Je vais passer deux semaines à la campagne. **II.** J'ai envie de manger maintenant. Je mange quand j'ai faim. Je bois quand j'ai soif. J'ai l'habitude de manger chez moi. **III.** Il y a deux parcs dans cette ville. Il y a un parc près de ma maison. Je joue à la balle et je joue au tennis dans un parc. **IV.** 1. Ils courent. 2. C'est un gâteau. 3. Elle joue à la balle.

DEVOIR 7

II. 1. heure 2. est 3. quelle 4. heures 5. le **III.** 1. Il est une heure (il est deux heures, *etc.*). 2. Je prends le petit déjeuner à sept heures. 3. Je prends le déjeuner à une heure. 4. Je prends le dîner à sept heures. 5. Je me couche à dix heures tous les soirs. **IV.** heure, me, et, vais, classe, demie, ai, chez, trois **V.** 1. Il est une heure. 2. Il est deux heures et demie. **VI.** Je vais à la classe de français à trois heures. J'ai rendez-vous chez le dentiste à quatre heures. **VII.** 1. Je vais à la classe de français à une heure. 2. Je vais chez le dentiste à trois heures. 3. Je vais chez moi à quatre heures. **VIII.** La date: le premier octobre. L'heure: deux heures. Madame Durand a rendez-vous à trois heures mais elle arrive à quatre heures.

DEVOIR 8

II. 1. un 2. la 3. à 4. à 5. faut **III.** 1. On regarde des objets d'art dans un musée. 2. On lit dans une bibliothèque. 3. On apprend à l'école. 4. Il faut étudier pour apprendre. 5. On va à la gare pour prendre un train. **IV.** 1. On regarde des objets d'art. 2. On lit. 3. On achète des billets. **V.** 1. Le prix du billet est cent quarante-huit francs. (Consult the section on Numbers in the back pages of this book). 2. Je pars de Rennes. 3. Je vais à Paris. 4. J'arrive à la Gare Montparnasse. 5. Je voyage en deuxième classe. 6. C'est pour une personne adulte. 7. C'est pour deux enfants. 8. Il est utilisable du 22 octobre au 21 décembre.

DEVOIR 9

II. 1. au 2. en 3. la 4. haute 5. basse. **III.** 1. au bas de la page dix-huit. 2. en haut de la page vingt. 3. à la page quinze. 4. à haute voix (à voix basse) 5. Je m'appelle (plus your name). **IV.** 1. en haut de 2. à voix basse 3. termine 4. à gauche **V.** au bas de la page dix-huit, en haut de la page vingt, je lis à la page quinze maintenant, je réponds au professeur à haute voix (à voix basse). **VI.** 1. DEMAIN 2. POUR 3. VINGT 4. PAGE 5. QUINZE 6. DEVOIR **VII.** C'est un livre.

REVIEW TEST 3

I. Je vais à la classe de français à une heure. J'ai rendez-vous chez le dentiste à trois heures et demie. **II.** On regarde des objets d'art dans un musée. On lit dans une bibliothèque. On achète des billets dans une gare. On apprend à l'école. **III.** Le devoir pour demain commence au bas de la page dix-huit. Il se termine en haut de la page vingt. Je lis à la page quinze maintenant. **IV.** 1. C'est un livre. 2. Il est quatre heures. 3. Il est sept heures et demie. 4. Le prix du billet est cent soixante-dix francs. 5. Je pars de Lyon. 6. Je vais à Paris. 7. J'arrive à la Gare de Lyon. 8. Je voyage en deuxième classe. 9. Pour deux personnes adultes. 10. Pour un (une) enfant.

DEVOIR 10

II. La date: le premier octobre. Chère Monique, Je m'appelle (plus your name). J'ai (number) ans. Je me lève à six heures et demie. Tous les matins je prends un bon petit déjeuner. J'écris en français. Amicalement (plus your name). **III.** 1. J'ai l'intention d'écrire une lettre en français cet après-midi. 2. A cette heure mon meilleur ami (ma meilleure amie) est chez le (la) dentiste. 3. Chaque soir après le dîner j'aime regarder la télé. 4. J'aime les bananes, les cerises (cherries), et les framboises (raspberries). (Consult the Review of Basic Vocabulary by Topics in the Appendix). 5. Nous sommes vendredi, le vingt-six octobre. **IV.** 1. C'est samedi, le 22 novembre. 2. Jacqueline Pucelle écrit la lettre. 3. Elle désire le catalogue de BICYCLETTES MODERNES. 4. Pour participer au Tour de France. 5. C'est 10, rue des Jardins, Paris.

DEVOIR 11

II. 1. demeure 2. trouve 3. de 4. en 5. de **III.** 1. Je demeure dans une grande maison. 2. Elle se trouve près d'ici. 3. Oui. Il y a beaucoup de fleurs dans notre jardin. 4. De temps en temps je travaille dans le jardin. 5. A côté de chez nous il y a de bons voisins. **IV.** 1. un robinet (a faucet) 2. un radiateur (a radiator) 3. le séchoir (dryer); (la plomberie, le chauffage, l'électricité). **V.** 1. C'est une maison. 2. C'est une lampe.

DEVOIR 12

II. 1. lave 2. de 3. brosse 4. me 5. habille **III.** 1. Oui. Je me lave tous les matins. 2. Oui. Je me lave avant de quitter la maison. 3. Oui. Je me brosse les dents tous les matins. 4. Oui. Je me brosse les cheveux. 5. Je m'habille dans ma chambre. **IV.** A. 1. se laver 2. se brosser les dents 3. se brosser les cheveux (Consult the section on 115 verbs used in this book in the Appendix). B. 1. la mère 2. le petit garçon 3. les mains

REVIEW TEST 4

I. La date: le trois octobre. Chère Monique, Je m'appelle (plus your name). J'ai (number) ans. Je me lève à six heures et demie. Tous les matins je prends un bon petit déjeuner. J'écris en français. Amicalement (plus your name). **II.** Je demeure dans une grande (petite) maison. Elle se trouve près d'ici. Il y a beaucoup de fleurs dans notre (mon) jardin. A côté de chez nous (moi) il y a de bons voisins. **III.** 1. la lampe 2. la radio 3. le radiateur 4. le robinet **IV.** 1. vous (toi) 2. quelle 3. que c'est 4. écrit 5. désire 6. grande (petite) 7. travaille 8. brosse 9. chambre 10. matins (jours) **V.** 1. laves 2. me 3. matins 4. brosses 5. cheveux (dents)

DEVOIR 13

II. 1. faire 2. faire 3. faut 4. bonne 5. coucher **III.** 1. Je vais faire un voyage. 2. Il faut faire la malle tout de suite. 3. Il faut faire les valises aussi. 4. Il faut me lever de bonne heure parce que (because) je vais faire un voyage. 5. Il faut me coucher de bonne heure parce que je vais me lever de bonne heure. **IV.** 1. C'est un train. 2. C'est un bateau. **V.** A. 1. les vêtements (clothing) 2. les articles de toilette (Consult the Review of Basic Vocabulary by Topics in the Appendix). B. 1. faire un voyage 2. faire la valise 3. faire la malle **VI.** Demain je vais faire un voyage. Il faut faire la malle tout de suite. Il faut faire les valises aussi.

DEVOIR 14

II. 1. ai 2. avez 3. ai 4. avez 5. faire **III.** 1. Quand j'ai chaud j'ouvre la fenêtre (je bois un jus d'orange/I drink an orange juice). 2. Quand j'ai froid je ferme la fenêtre (je bois une tasse de thé chaud/I drink a hot cup of tea). 3. Quand j'ai sommeil je dors (I sleep/to sleep, dormir). 4. Quand il pleut j'ai besoin d'un parapluie (umbrella). 5. Mon premier repas du jour est le petit déjeuner.
IV. 1. la femme 2. être malade 3. avoir 4. de la fièvre 5. le médecin 6. le lit

DEVOIR 15

II. 1. amuse 2. fais 3. voiture 4. promenade 5. du **III.** 1. Je m'amuse le samedi (le vendredi, *etc.*).
2. J'aime faire une promenade le long du fleuve (dans un parc, *etc.*). 3. Oui. Je sais jouer du violon (Non. Je ne sais pas jouer de violon). 4. Je vais au cinéma (Je vais au parc, *etc.*). 5. Je joue à la balle (Je joue au tennis, *etc.*). **IV.** 1. Il fait une promenade. 2. Elle fait une promenade. **V.** Je fais une promenade. Je fais une promenade en voiture. Je joue du violon et du piano. Je vais au cinéma. Je regarde la télé. **VI.** 1. me 2. ne 3. nom 4. de **VII.** 1. le 2. fais (sais) 3. joue (pour) 4. fait

REVIEW TEST 5

I. C'est un bateau. **II.** Je vais faire un voyage demain. Il faut faire la malle tout de suite. Il faut faire les valises aussi. **III.** Madame Durand est malade. Elle a de la fièvre. Elle est dans le lit. Le médecin est à côté d'elle (à côté du lit). **IV.** 1. Je m'amuse le samedi (le vendredi, *etc.*). 2. Demain je vais faire un voyage. 3. Quand j'ai sommeil je dors. **V.** 1. Il fait une promenade. 2. Elle fait une promenade.
VI. A. 1. les vêtements 2. les articles de toilette B. 1. faire un voyage 2. faire la valise 3. faire la malle C. 1. jouer 2. regarder 3. la télé 4. cinéma **VII.** 1. vais (sais) 2. joue (pour) 3. le (me) 4. vais (bois)
VIII. 1. vais 2. ai, fièvre 3. promenade

DEVOIR 16

II. 1. mangeons 2. voyons 3. allons **III.** A. 1. l'homme 2. mange 3. beaucoup 4. gros (fat) 5. l'appétit 6. le gâteau **IV.** 1. Nous chantons dans notre club. 2. Les réunions ont lieu tous les vendredis.
3. Nous allons en ville de temps en temps. 4. De temps en temps nous mangeons dans un restaurant français. 5. Nous voyons des films français.

DEVOIR 17

II. 1. que 2. avez 3. ai 4. avez 5. ne **III.** A. 1. avoir l'air triste 2. avoir honte 3. l'agent de police 4. le ballon 5. casser (to break) 6. la vitre (window pane) B. 1. la question 2. heureux (heureuse), content (contente) 3. rien 4. avoir raison **IV.** La date: le premier novembre. Cher ami Gérard (Chère amie Michelle), Merci mille fois pour le basket-ball. Je suis très content(e). Amitiés (Write your name).

DEVOIR 18

II. 1. depuis 2. de 3. des 4. pose 5. à **III.** 1. la maîtresse de français 2. le bureau 3. la chaise 4. le globe 5. le tableau 6. la salle de classe **IV.** 1. J'étudie le français depuis un an (deux ans, trois ans, *etc.*) 2. Oui. Je vais continuer à étudier le français l'année prochaine. J'aime beaucoup le français. 3. Je parle, je lis, et j'écris en français. **V.** à l'école, j'étudie le français depuis deux ans, je vais continuer à étudier le français l'année prochaine, merci bien, au revoir

REVIEW TEST 6

I. 1. la salle de classe 2. la maîtresse de français 3. le bureau 4. la chaise 5. le globe 6. le tableau
II. 1. Je ne sais pas la réponse. (Remember that in this section, and in others in all the Devoirs and Review Tests, there is not only one answer in French. Many answers given are sample answers. You are doing fine as long as what you write in French answers the question and makes sense.) 2. Le contraire de l'expression *avoir tort* est *avoir raison*. 3. Nous chantons dans notre club (Je chante dans mon club). 4. Les réunions de notre (mon) club ont lieu tous les vendredis (tous les lundis, *etc.*). 5. Nous voyons (Je vois) des films français. **III.** 1. mangeons 2. allons 3. voyons 4. depuis 5. classe **IV.** à l'école, j'étudie le français depuis deux ans, je vais continuer à étudier le français l'année prochaine, merci bien, au revoir **V.** 1. la question. 2. heureux (heureuse), content (contente) 3. rien 4. avoir raison

DEVOIR 19

II. 1. de 2. habitude 3. face 4. fait 5. heure

III.

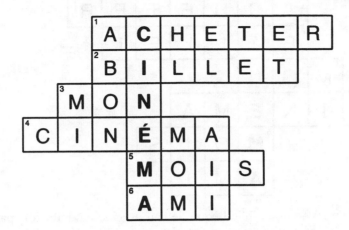

IV. 1. D'habitude je vais au cinéma deux fois (une fois, *etc.*) par mois. 2. Je vais au cinéma avec mes amis. 3. Le cinéma est en face de la bibliothèque. 4. Mon ami achète les billets. 5. Nous arrivons toujours à l'heure au cinéma. **V.** Je vais au cinéma, c'est en face de la bibliothèque, je vais au cinéma deux fois par mois.

DEVOIR 20

II. 1. ne 2. aucun 3. ne 4. rien 5. ne **III.** 1. Je ne vois personne. 2. Je n'ai aucun frère (Je n'ai pas de frères). 3. Je ne vois rien. 4. Je n'ai jamais été en Chine.

IV.

V. 1. rien 2. personne 3. jamais 4. quelque chose **VI.** 1. Paul ne parle à personne. 2. Il n'a aucun ami. 3. Il ne vient plus chez nous (chez moi). 4. Il ne me dit rien. 5. Je ne lui parlerai jamais!

DEVOIR 21

II. 1. temps 2. faire 3. à 4. sers 5. la **III.** 1. Il faut faire attention en classe pour apprendre. 2. Cette année nous commençons à écrire en français. 3. Pour écrire, je me sers d'un stylo et de papier.
IV. Elle écrit une lettre. **V.** 1. C'est la Papeterie Royale. 2. L'adresse est 129, Avenue Royale, Paris. 3. Le numéro de téléphone est quarante-trois, quatre-vingt-douze, soixante-six, vingt-neuf (Consult the section on Numbers in the Appendix). 4. Les prix sont bas (The prices are low). 5. Du papier (some paper), un cahier (a notebook), une règle (a ruler), un stylo (a pen), un crayon (a pencil), une gomme (an eraser).

REVIEW TEST 7

I. D'habitude je vais au cinéma deux fois par mois. Le cinéma est en face de la bibliothèque. J'arrive toujours à l'heure au cinéma.

II.

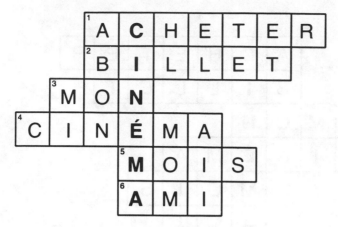

III. Je vais au cinéma, c'est en face de la bibliothèque, je vais au cinéma deux fois par mois.
IV. 1. Paul ne parle à personne. 2. Il n'a aucun ami. 3. Il ne vient plus chez nous (chez moi). 4. Il ne me dit rien. 5. Je ne lui parlerai jamais! **V.** Elle écrit une lettre. **VI.** 1. C'est la Papeterie Royale. 2. L'adresse est 129, Avenue Royale, Paris. 3. Le numéro de téléphone est quarante-trois, quatre-vingt-douze, soixante-six, vingt-neuf (Consult the section on Numbers in the Appendix; you must practice writing out numbers in French words). 4. Les prix sont bas (The prices are low). 5. Du papier (some paper), un cahier (a notebook), une règle (a ruler), un stylo (a pen), un crayon (a pencil), une gomme (an eraser).

DEVOIR 22

II. 1. de 2. rendre 3. à 4. veux 5. lieu **III.** 1. Mon père vient de quitter la maison. 2. Il va rendre visite à mon oncle. 3. Mon père ressemble à mon oncle. 4. Oui. Je veux bien aller avec mon père. 5. Non. Je vais avec mon père pour voir mon oncle. **IV.** La date: le premier décembre. Cher cousin Pierre (Chère cousine Madeleine), Mon père vient de quitter la maison. Il va rendre visite à mon oncle. Au lieu de rester à la maison, je veux bien y aller avec lui. Bien à toi (Write your name). **V.** 1. VENIR 2. VOULOIR 3. RESTER 4. RESSEMBLER 5. RENDRE 6. ALLER **VI.** 1. ma 2. mai 3. mais 4. mois 5. on 6. son

DEVOIR 23

II. 1. quelque 2. milieu 3. quelle 4. à 5. de **III.** 1. Hier j'ai vu un clown. 2. au milieu de la rue 3. J'ai éclaté de rire. 4. Il était jaune. 5. Mes chaussures sont blanches. **IV.** 1. J'ai vu un clown. 2. au milieu de la rue 3. J'ai éclaté de rire. **V.** Rien **VI.** La lettre *r*. **VII.** 1. Je préfère 2. cinéma 3. un film intéressant 4. une histoire d'amour

DEVOIR 24

II. 1. est 2. bon 3. trouve 4. cher **III.** 1. C'est un stylo. 2. dans une papeterie 3. là-bas, de l'autre côté de la rue 4. Je n'ai pas payé cher (Je l'ai acheté bon marché). **IV.** J'ai acheté un stylo. Il est noir. J'ai acheté le stylo dans une papeterie. La boutique se trouve là-bas, de l'autre côté de la rue. Je n'ai pas payé cher. **V.** 1. désirer 2. acheter 3. un stylo 4. bon marché **VI.** 1. être 2. acheter 3. se trouve 4. payer **VII.** 1. être à 2. de bon coeur 3. de l'autre côté 4. bon marché **VIII.** 1. coeur 2. qui

REVIEW TEST 8

I. 1. Mon père vient de quitter la maison. 2. Il va rendre visite à mon oncle. 3. Mon père ressemble à mon oncle. 4. Oui. Je veux bien aller avec mon père. 5. Non. Je vais avec mon père pour voir mon oncle. **II.** La date: le trois décembre. Cher cousin René (Chère cousine Renée), Mon père vient de quitter la maison. Il va rendre visite à mon oncle. Au lieu de rester à la maison, je veux bien y aller avec lui. Bien à toi (Write your name). **III.** 1. J'ai vu un clown. 2. au milieu de la rue 3. J'ai éclaté de rire. **IV.** Rien **V.** La lettre *r*. **VI.** 1. Je préfère 2. cinéma 3. un film intéressant 4. une histoire d'amour **VII.** 1. C'est un stylo. 2. dans une papeterie 3. là-bas, de l'autre côté de la rue 4. Je n'ai pas payé cher (Je l'ai acheté bon marché). **VIII.** 1. désirer (vouloir) 2. acheter 3. un stylo 4. bon marché

DEVOIR 25

II. 1. dernière 2. fait 3. suis 4. peine 5. pas **III.** 1. se faire mal 2. se casser 3. aller 4. écrire **IV.** 1. se faire mal 2. à peine **V.** 1. semaine 2. suis 3. fait 4. cassé 5. peux 6. médecin 7. de 8. pas **VI.** 1. se faire mal 2. se casser une jambe (leg) 3. un bras (arm) 4. aller mieux **VII.** La date: le premier décembre. Cher ami Louis (Chère amie Louise), La semaine dernière je me suis cassé un doigt. Je peux à peine écrire. Je suis allé(e) voir un médecin. Le médecin m'a dit de ne pas écrire. A bientôt (Write your name).

DEVOIR 26

II. 1. ai 2. en 3. y 4. fin 5. de **III.** 1. Oui. Hier j'ai assité à un mariage. 2. Non. Je suis arrivé(e) en retard à la cérémonie. 3. Il y avait cent personnes. 4. A la fin de la cérémonie, je suis allé(e) (nous sommes allés) dîner. 5. J'ai mangé (Nous avons mangé) de bon appétit. **IV.** 1. assisté 2. allé(e)(s) 3. arrivé(e)(s) 4. mangé **V.** 1. Hier j'ai assisté à un mariage (J'ai assisté à un mariage hier). 2. Il y avait cent personnes. **VI.** 1. une batterie de cuisine 2. une marmite 3. un vase 4. une lampe

DEVOIR 27

II. 1. faut 2. ai 3. par 4. ai 5. entendu **III.** 1. les enfants et le petit chien 2. regarder la télé 3. avoir peur 4. la violence **IV.** 1. avoir peur 2. avoir raison 3. avoir tort 4. avoir lieu (Consult the section Review of Basic French Idioms with **aller, avoir, être, faire** in the Appendix). **V.** Salut, Jacqueline! Comment vas-tu? Qu'est-ce que tu désires? (Qu'est-ce que tu veux?). Quel cinéma? Non, parce que j'ai peur de traverser le parc la nuit. C'est bien dangereux. Je préfère samedi prochain dans l'après-midi. D'accord (Okay). Au revoir.

REVIEW TEST 9

I. 1. semaine 2. suis 3. fait 4. cassé 5. peux 6. médecin 7. de 8. pas **II.** 1. se faire mal 2. se casser une jambe (leg) 3. un bras (arm) 4. aller mieux **III.** La date: le quinze décembre. Cher ami Yves (Chère amie Yvette), La semaine dernière je me suis cassé un doigt. Je peux à peine écrire. Je suis allé(e) voir un médecin. Le médecin m'a dit de ne pas écrire. A bientôt (Write your name). **IV.** 1. un chien 2. un homme 3. avoir peur 4. courir **V.** Salut, Jacqueline! Comment vas-tu? Qu'est-ce que tu désires? (Qu'est-ce que tu veux?). Quel cinéma? Non, parce que j'ai peur de traverser le parc la nuit. C'est bien dangereux. Je préfère samedi prochain dans l'après-midi. D'accord (Okay). Au revoir.

DEVOIR 28

II. 1. plus 2. au 3. en 4. suis 5. me **III.** (a) Samedi j'ai travaillé du matin au soir. (b) Dimanche je me suis reposé(e) (Je me suis reposé(e) dimanche). (c) Aujourd'hui je me porte beaucoup mieux.
IV.

```
 1                 2              3              4
[D][O][N][N][É][ ][ ][L][ ][ ][ ][V]
[Û][ ][ ][ ][É][ ][ ][P][U][ ][ ][E]   5
[ ][ ][D][ ][ ][ ][ ][R][ ][ ][ ][N]   6
 7                 8              9
[F][U][I][ ][ ][R][I][ ][ ][Û][D]
[A][ ][T][U][ ][ ][S][U][ ][ ][U]      10  11 12
 13                14             15
[L][U][ ][ ][F][ ][ ][S][U][ ][ ]
[L][ ][M][ ][ ][I][ ][ ][É][ ][É]      16        17
[U][ ][O][ ][ ][N][É][ ][ ][T]         18
[ ][I][R][ ][ ][I][ ][ ][E][ ][É]      19        20
[ ][T][U][ ][ ][T][U][É]               21     22
```

DEVOIR 29

II. 1. ce 2. suis 3. dommage 4. le 5. ai **III.** 1. Qu'est-ce qui est arrivé? 2. se blesser 3. dommage 4. aller mieux **IV.** Bonjour, Monique! Je me suis blessée dans un accident. Dans un accident de voiture. Tout le monde me pose la même question! Non, ce n'est pas grave (Rien de grave). Tout va bien maintenant. Merci.

DEVOIR 30

II. 1. demandé 2. refusé 3. eu 4. fait 5. demande **III.** 1. D'habitude, je demande de l'argent à mon père. 2. Mon père m'a donné cent francs (Il a eu la bonté de me donner cent francs). 3. J'ai fait des emplettes. **IV.** J'ai demandé de l'argent à mon père. Il a eu la bonté de me donner cent francs. J'ai fait des emplettes. **V. A.** 1. Madame Durand 2. faire des emplettes 3. le magasin 4. l'argent **B.** 1. un nouveau manteau (a new coat) 2. de nouvelles bottes (new boots). 3. une jolie robe (a pretty dress) 4. un chemisier (a blouse). (Use the vocabulary pages in the Appendix for other words you prefer to use). **VI.** 1. des fruits 2. des pâtisseries 3. de la laitue 4. des oeufs 5. des brioches 6. du lait (If you prefer to write other foods in French, consult the Review of Basic Vocabulary by Topics and the vocabulary pages in the Appendix).

REVIEW TEST 10

I. (a) Samedi j'ai travaillé du matin au soir. (b) Dimanche je me suis reposé(e). (c) Aujourd'hui je me porte beaucoup mieux. **II.** J'ai demandé de l'argent à mon père. Il a eu la bonté de me donner cent francs. J'ai fait des emplettes. **III. A.** 1. Madame Dupont 2. faire des emplettes 3. le grand magasin 4. l'argent **B.** 1. un nouveau manteau (a new coat) 2. de nouvelles bottes (new boots) 3. une jolie robe (a pretty dress) 4. un chemisier (a blouse) **IV.** 1. Qu'est-ce qui est arrivé? 2. se blesser 3. dommage 4. aller mieux **V.** Bonjour, Monique! Je me suis blessée dans un accident. Dans un accident de voiture. Tout le monde me pose la même question! Non, ce n'est pas grave (Rien de grave). Tout va bien maintenant. Merci.

DEVOIR 31

II. 1. y 2. anniversaire 3. me 4. reçu 5. avons **III.** 1. Je suis né(e) le (plus date and month). 2. J'ai célébré mon anniversaire de naissance à la maison 3. J'ai reçu un vélo (or whatever you would like to state). **IV. A.** 1. dans la rue 2. dans un parc 3. sur une piste (on a path) 4. sur un chemin (on a road). **B.** 1. beau 2. grand 3. nouveau (new) 4. rouge (red). **V.** La date: le 5 avril. Cher ami David (Chère amie Odette), J'ai célébré mon anniversaire de naissance à la maison le premier avril (or whatever date you give). J'ai reçu un vélo pour mon anniversaire (or any other gift you prefer to mention). Nous avons chanté et dansé jusqu'à minuit. A bientôt (Write your name).

DEVOIR 32

II. 1. est 2. est 3. est 4. sont 5. doute **III.** 1. Une dame est sortie d'une boulangerie. 2. Elle s'est arrêtée devant la boutique. 3. Une autre dame s'est approchée d'elle. **IV. A.** 1. sortir (de) 2. s'arrêter 3. s'approcher (de) 4. se mettre (à) **B.** 1. du pain 2. des petits pains (rolls) **C.** 1. le chien (dog) 2. manger 3. le gâteau 4. avoir faim (Consult the Review of Basic Vocabulary by Topics and the vocabulary in the Appendix).

DEVOIR 33

II. 1. La petite fille a mis le nouveau chapeau de sa mère. 2. Sa mère est entrée dans la chambre tout à coup. 3. Sa mère s'est fâchée. 4. Elle a commencé à pleurer tout de suite. 5. A l'instant la mère a mis le chapeau dans la boîte. **III.** 1. deux petites filles 2. des petites robes d'été 3. faciles à porter (easy to wear) 4. joli(e)(s) 5. le grand magazin 6. en rose, en bleu

REVIEW TEST 11

I. A. 1. dans la rue 2. dans un parc 3. sur une piste (on a path) 4. sur un chemin (on a road) **B.** 1. beau 2. grand 3. nouveau (new) 4. rouge (red). **II.** Cher ami Joseph (Chère amie Joséphine), J'ai célébré mon anniversaire de naissance à la maison le premier avril (or give your birth date). J'ai reçu un vélo pour mon anniversaire (or any gift you prefer to mention). Nous avons chanté et dansé jusqu'à minuit. A bientôt (Write your name). (Consult the Appendix for a variety of vocabulary, verbs, and other useful sections). **III.** 1. Une dame 2. Devant une boulangerie 3. Une autre dame **IV.** 1. La petite fille 2. La mère 3. La mère 4. Elle a pleuré. 5. Elle a mis le chapeau dans la boîte. **V. A.** 1. du pain 2. des petits pains **B.** 1. le chien 2. manger 3. le gâteau 4. avoir faim

DEVOIR 34

II. 1. fait 2. suis 3. tu 4. pas 5. A **III.** 1. à l'école 2. à l'opéra (au concert) 3. le piano, le violon **IV. A.** 1. à l'opéra 2. au théâtre **B.** 1. l'acteur 2. un roi 3. la scène (the stage) 4. le théâtre **V.** La date: le premier mai. Cher ami Jean (Chère amie Janine), J'ai fait la connaissance de beaucoup de personnes ici à Paris. Je suis allé(e) à l'opéra. A propos, aimes-tu l'opéra? N'oublie pas d'écrire. A bientôt (Write your name).

DEVOIR 35

II. 1. à 2. pas 3. tout 4. de 5. par **III.** 1. à ce poème 2. J'ai appris par coeur le poème français *Les Oiseaux (The Birds)*. 3. (a) Il n'y a pas de fumée sans feu *(Where there is smoke there is fire)*. (This is found at the end of Review Test 2). (b) Qui ne risque rien n'a rien *(Nothing ventured, nothing gained)*. (This is found at the end of Review Test 3). (c) Plus ça change, plus c'est la même chose *(The more it changes, the more it remains the same)*. (This is found at the end of Review Test 4). Note that there is a French proverb with English equivalent at the end of each Review Test. **IV.** 1. faire un voyage **V.** 1. beau 2. intelligent 3. un pull, un pullover (sweater) 4. de beaux cheveux **VI.** 1. penser 2. se 3. sur 4. ne 5. rue 6. peur

DEVOIR 36

II. 1. ça 2. tout 3. suis 4. à 5. revoir **III.** 1. à Paris. 2. deux 3. deux 4. grand 5. quarante-cinq, zéro quatre, cinquante-cinq, quatorze (You must practice writing out numbers in French words; consult the section on Numbers in the Appendix). **IV. A.** 1. la carte d'accès à bord 2. le vol 3. l'embarquement *(m)* 4. la correspondance 5. la porte 6. le siège **B.** 1. à quelle heure? 2. c'est combien? 3. partir 4. l'avion *(m)* **C.** 1. à 13 h. (heures) 25 (1:25 PM) 2. 23-H

REVIEW TEST 12

I. La date: le quinze mai. Cher ami Jacques (Chère amie Jacqueline), J'ai fait la connaissance de beaucoup de personnes ici à Paris. Je suis allé(e) à l'opéra. A propos, aimes-tu l'opéra? N'oublie pas d'écrire. A bientôt (Write your name). **II.** 1. à une carte postale à mon ami(e) (Or anything else you prefer to write). 2. *Les Oiseaux (The Birds)* 3. (a) Il n'y a pas de fumée sans feu. (b) Qui ne risque rien n'a rien. (c) Plus ça change, plus c'est la même chose. **III.** 1. ça 2. tout 3. suis 4. à 5. revoir **IV. A.** 1. la carte d'accès à bord 2. le vol 3. l'embarquement *(m)* 4. la correspondance 5. la porte 6. le siège **B.** 1. à quelle heure? 2. c'est combien? 3. partir 4. arriver **C.** 1. 13:25 (1:25 PM) 2. 23-H 3. Non. C'est direct. 4. zéro, soixante-dix-sept 5. Je pars de New York et je vais à Paris.

DEVOIR 37

II. 1. dans 2. cet 3. ça et là 4. aller **III.** 1. faire la valise 2. faire la malle 3. faire un voyage 4. les vêtements (clothes) 5. les articles de toilette 6. aller en vacances **IV.** 1. Je préfère 2. nager (to swim) 3. jouer 4. sur la plage (on the beach) **V.** 1. aller en vacances 2. un maillot de bain (swim suit) 3. bon marché 4. une carte de crédit

DEVOIR 38

II. 1. suis, au 2. mal 3. suis 4. de 5. par

III.

DEVOIR 39

II. 1. Il est président d'une banque (il est avocat, *etc.*). 2. huit heures. 3. J'écoute. **III.** 1. mon père 2. aller 3. travailler 4. en retard 5. oublier 6. son pantalon 7. une tasse de café 8. l'autobus

DEVOIR 40

II. 1. dit 2. aime 3. dire 4. rien 5. quoi 6. prie 7. revoir 8. veut

III.

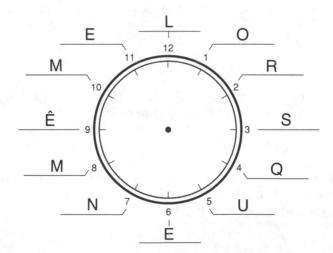

IV. 1. Elle ne me les donne pas. 2. Je ne le leur donne pas. 3. Ne les leur donnez pas. 4. Elle ne s'est pas lavée. 5. Je ne le lui ai pas donné. (If you need to understand the correct order of words in these sentences, you must consult the section on Sentence Structure in the Appendix).

REVIEW TEST 13

I. 1. faire la valise 2. faire la malle 3. faire un voyage 4. les vêtements 5. aller en vacances 6. deux semaines **II.** 1. Je préfère 2. nager 3. jouer 4. sur la plage **III.** 1. Il est président d'une banque. 2. sept heures 3. J'écoute. **IV.** 1. Elle ne me les donne pas. 2. Je ne le leur donne pas. 3. Ne les leur donnez pas. 4. Elle ne s'est pas lavée. 5. Je ne le lui ai pas donné. **V.** 1. dit 2. aime 3. dire 4. rien 5. quoi 6. prie 7. revoir 8. veut **VI.** 1. aller en vacances 2. un maillot de bain 3. une carte de crédit 4. bon marché

notes

notes

notes

notes

notes